Family Fun in Thailand

– the best tourist attractions in the most popular holiday destinations in Thailand

ERIC ARCHER

Family Fun in Thailand
– the best tourist attractions in the most popular holiday destinations in Thailand

Asia Revealed Publishing Company

Copy Right Asia Revealed Publishing Company
All rights reserved. No textual part of this publication may be reproduced, stored in a retrieval system, or transmitted, in any form or by any means, without the prior permission in writing from the publisher, nor be otherwise circulated in any form of binding or cover other than that in which it is published without a similar condition of approval.

©2017 by Asia Revealed Publishing Company
Publisher: Asia Revealed Publishing Company, Weston-super-Mare, United Kingdom
Pictures: All photos in this publication have been released under Creative Commons CCO, including for commercial purposes
Print: Ingram Content Group/Lightning Source
ISBN: 978-1-912414-00-0

Content

Preface 13

Bangkok 15

    Art in Paradise 16

    Bounce 16

    Children's Discovery Museum 17

    Dinosaur Planet 18

    Dream World 19

    Dusit Zoo 20

    Escape Rooms Bangkok 20

    Fantasia Lagoon/Paradise Water Park 22

    Fishing 23

    Flow House Bangkok 23

    Funarium 24

    Harbin Ice Wonderland 25

    Imaginia Playland & Benjasiri Park 26

    Ice-skating 27

    KidZania 27

    Leoland Water Park & Mega Bangna 29

    Lumpini Park 29

    Madame Tussauds 30

    Safari World 31

    Samut Prakarn Crocodile Farm and Zoo 32

    Sea Life Bangkok Ocean World 33

Siam Niramit Show 34
Snake Farm 35
Snow Town & Kidzoona 36
Suan Siam Water Park/Siam Park City 37
Wakeboarding 37
Yoyo Land 38
Chiang Mai 40
Art in Paradise 41
Caves and Caving 41
Muang On Cave 42
Chiang Dao Caves 42
Central Festival: Ice-skating and Shopping 43
Chiang Mai X-Center 43
Chiang Mai Zoo & Aquarium 44
Chiang Mai Zoo 45
Chiang Mai Aquarium 45
Doi Suthep 46
Elephant Farms 47
Elephant Nature Park 47
Patara Elephant Farm 48
Mae Sa Elephant Camp 48
Flight of the Gibbon: Ziplining 49
Flights over Chiang Mai 50
Jungle Bungy Jump 50

Mae Sa Snake Farm 51

Mini-Golf 52

    Inter Mini-Golf 52

    Hansa Mini-Golf: Discover the World of Wonders 52

Night Safari 53

Night Bazaar 54

Queen Sirikit Botanic Garden 55

Rivers of Chiang Mai 55

    White Water Rafting 56

    Bamboo Rafting 56

Segways in Chiang Mai 57

Swimming and Water Play 57

    The Waterfalls of Chiang Mai 57

    San Kamphaeng Hot Springs 58

Tiger Kingdom 59

Tubing on Mae Ping River 60

Hua Hin and Cha-Am 61

    Beach Activities 62

    Black Mountain Mini-Golf & Wakeboard Park 62

    Black Sheep Farm 63

    Boating and Fishing Trips 64

    Camel Republic Cha-Am 65

    Cha-Am ATV Park 66

    Go Kart Hua Hin 67

Hua Hin Horse Club 67

Hua Hin Safari & Adventure Park 68

Huai Sai Wildlife Breeding Center 69

Hutsadin Elephant Foundation 70

Khao Takiab and the Monkey Temple 71

Magic Balloon Park 71

Markets and Shopping Malls in Hua Hin 72

    Hua Hin Night Market & Chatsila Night Market 72

    Cicada Market 73

    Grand Market Hua Hin 73

    Plaern Wan Shopping Village 74

    Hua Hin Market Village 74

    Blu'Port – Hua Hin Resort Mall 75

National Parks 76

    The Waterfalls of Pala-U 76

    Khao Sam Roi Yot 77

Palapon Martial Arts & Holistic Fitness Camp 78

Paramotor Flying Hua Hin 78

Santorini Park Cha-Am 79

Sam Phan Nam Floating Market 80

Swiss Sheep Farm Cha-Am 80

The Venezia 81

Waghor Aquarium 82

Water Parks 83

Black Mountain Water Park 83
Santorini Water Fantasy 84
Vana Nava Hua Hin Water Park 84
Phuket 86
   Animal Shows 87
   Elephant Trekking 87
   Fishing 88
   Horse Riding 89
      Phuket International Horse Club 89
   Island Hopping 89
   Kids Club Phuket / Kee Resort and Spa 90
   Mini-Golf in Phuket 90
      Mini-Golf at Dino Park 91
      Football Crazy Golf 91
      Phuket Adventure Mini-Golf 92
   Museums in Phuket 92
      Thalang National Museum 92
      Phuket Mining Museum in Kathu 93
      Phuket Seashell Museum 93
   Paramotor Flying Phuket 94
   Patong Go-Kart Speed Way 95
   Phuket Aquarium 95
   Phuket Bird Park 96
   Phuket FantaSea 97

Phuket Trickeye Museum 97
Shopping Malls 98
    Jungceylon Shopping Mall 98
    Central Festival Phuket 99
Siam Niramit Show 100
Splash Jungle Water Park 100
Surf House Phuket 101
Tiger Kingdom Phuket 102
Upside-Down House: Baan Teelanka 103
Wakeboarding 103
    Phuket Wake Park 104
    Anthem Wake Park 104
White Water Rafting 105
Ziplining: Flying Hanuman & Jungle Xtrem Adventure Park 106
Zorbing at Rollerball 106

Asia Revealed Publishing Company

Preface

There is a lot to write about regarding traveling in Thailand. You could fill hundreds of pages with information about the many beaches, the best diving spots, the nicest coral reefs, and the most exciting boat trips. Similarly, you could fill another couple of hundred pages with information about the culture, the customs, and the religion. And yet another couple of hundred about the shopping and the bustling nightlife, not to mention the food and all the restaurants. The material must simply be reduced in order to become comprehensible. And in this book, all emphasis is put on activities and excursions that the whole family can enjoy together.

Most of the material can be found on the Internet; however, not always with ease, and the information differs in many cases between websites, thus creating confusion. Moreover, most websites about tourist attractions in Thailand are swamped with commercials, banners and ads, making it at times impossible to retrieve any relevant or trustworthy information. My aim with this book is, therefore, to remove everything unimportant or nonessential to present what there is to do, how much it costs and, more importantly, how to get there. A straightforward presentation about the things you really need to know when traveling in Thailand with children.

The costs and fees mentioned are dated to 2017. However, they sometimes change arbitrarily, and the meticulous traveler is advised to visit the websites of the listed places before setting out from the hotel. In a few cases, there will not be any specific websites connected to the presented activity; however, you will always be able to find a Facebook page. And although most of the destinations and attractions compiled in this book are fairly easy to access, it could also be worthwhile to jot down some information about directions and phone numbers, in case you get lost.

The cities presented are as follows: Bangkok, Chiang Mai, Hua Hin, Cha-Am, and Phuket. The activities for each place are listed in alphabetical order, respectively. In addition, almost all the places mentioned are so-called "permanent" installations. That is, considerable sums have been invested, and one does not have to worry about arriving at the attraction just to realize that is has shut down.

On a different note, there are certain moral issues involved in presenting, and indirect promoting, animal shows in Thailand. Many of them are beneath contempt, and occasionally horror stories of maltreatment of animals pop up in the local press. Nevertheless, a couple of animal shows figure in this book, but most of them are of a high standard, at least in comparison to the general state of affairs in this part of the world regarding zoos and animal farms. Tiger Kingdom in Chiang Mai and Phuket might, though, cause some visitors to feel slightly uneasy. Not due to neglect or abuse, but rather because it is impossible to release domesticated tigers into the wild. Moreover, the claim of some of the companies in this book to be fully certified and insured has not been confirmed, or verified, by anyone at Asia Revealed Publishing Company.

Asia Revealed Publishing Company

Bangkok

Bangkok is a city of contradictions and surprises.

On the one hand, it is one of the most modern and trendy capitals of Southeast Asia. On the other hand, it is a place firmly anchored in history. By just crossing the street, you can move from a neon sparkling shopping center to a blissful temple, and it is this peculiar mix of old and new that constitutes Bangkok's charm.

Despite being the home of over 10 million people, Bangkok rarely ever feels stressful or impersonal. The combination of modernity and ancient Buddhist traditions has created a place full of life and under the rough surface, which at first sight seems to be both chaotic and dangerous, you will find genuine hospitality, as well as open-mindedness. With the exception of the traffic situation, there are not that many perils an adventurous family would encounter in Bangkok, thus enabling an unreserved exploration of everything this fascinating city has got to offer.

When the Bangkokians take their families out for the weekend, they usually head to one of the numerous malls, often to escape the at times punishing heat and humidity. This has transformed many of the shopping centers in Bangkok to real tourist magnets. Here you can find everything from ice-skating rinks to enormous funfairs, mixed in with impressive water parks, and even small animal farms. Scattered over the many floors, there is an abundance of fun activities that will suit everyone in the family.

If not, you could always travel to the suburbs of Bangkok, where the really big amusement parks and zoos are located.

Art in Paradise

Art in Paradise is a gallery with interactive 3D paintings; however, not in the form of holograms, but rather in the guise of actual paintings. What it is about is creating the illusion of the beholder stepping into the artwork. The paintings are huge, sometimes covering entire walls, and offer amazing photo opportunities where oneself becomes part of the motif. Next to most of the paintings, there are instructions on how you should position yourself to best create the impression of being an integral part of the composition. The optical illusions are stunning, and the whole family will be fascinated by the end result when captured by your own camera.

At the venue, there is also a brand-new multimedia room where the visitors can learn about, and experiment with, various creative forums. As an added bonus, a trip to Art in Paradise can easily be combined with other fun activities as it is located in the shopping center The Esplanade, which, among other things, can boast a huge state-of-the-art skating rink.

Directions: The easiest way to get to Art in Paradise is by subway. Art in Paradise is located in the shopping mall The Esplanade, which lies a few hundred meters from the subway station Thailand Cultural Center.
Opening hours: Daily 09.00 – 21.00.
Admission fees: Adults 400 baht. Children 200 baht. Free admission for children under 100 cm.

Bounce

Advanced and innovative trampoline parks are becoming more and more popular all around the world, including Thailand, resulting in a company called Bounce setting up shop in two rather different shopping malls in Bangkok.

However, Bounce in Thailand, which started out as trampoline park for mainly young people, has evolved into a fitness and adventure park that suits people of all ages and fitness levels. Besides massive and elaborate trampolines, there are now also impressive climbing walls and Adventure Challenge Courses, constructed according to the concept of the extremely popular TV show "Ninja Warrior". Even the fittest people will find parts of these courses truly challenging, making a visit to Bounce fun for both adults and children.

Directions: The easiest way to get to Bounce at the shopping mall The Street is by subway. Just get off at Thailand Cultural Centre and walk a couple of hundred meters north of the station. If visiting Bounce at The Emporium, get off the skytrain at Phrom Phong station on the Sukhumvit Line.
Opening hours: Daily 10.00 – 22.00.
Admission fees: The cost starts at around 400 baht per person.

Children's Discovery Museum

The children's own discovery museum has been around for quite some time in Bangkok. However, a substantial sum was invested in the exhibitions in 2014, which raised the standard considerably. Now it is an innovative place for both young and old. There are enough entertaining activities to last the whole day. For example, you can learn about archaeology by digging out dinosaur bones in Dino Detective Park, or why not enter the science section and experiment with blowing up giant bubbles from within the actual bubbles. There are also several interactive displays about the human body and all its functions. In addition, the younger members of the family are invited to the section Build Our City, where they can construct their own miniature towns using various materials.

The Children's Discovery Museum is, simply put, a museum which allows children to touch and test instead of just passively watch and read. Moreover, outside the museum you will find a modern playground with an exciting labyrinth made of net, as well as a spouting fountains and shallow pools – bring your own towel and swimsuit. On the weekend, a trip to the Children's Discovery Museum can be combined with a visit to the famous outdoor market Chatuchak Weekend Market, which is one of the biggest in the world.

Directions: The easiest way to get to the Children's Discovery Museum is by skytrain or subway. If going by skytrain, get off at the end station Mor Chit on the Sukhumvit Line and walk approximately 200 meters towards the south end of Chatuchak Park. If going by subway, get off at Chatuchak Station, which is situated right next to Chatuchak Park.
Opening hours: Daily 10.00 – 16.00.
Admission fees: Free admission for both adults and children (minor fees can apply for certain activities).

Dinosaur Planet

After several years of construction work, and with over 500 million baht invested, Dinosaur Planet opened its doors to the public for the first time in 2015. The aim was to create the best edutainment place about dinosaurs in the whole of Southeast Asia, and on the premises, which is located in central Bangkok, the Thais' never-ending fascination of dinosaurs has now reach completely new levels.

Here you will find a dinosaur museum, shows about dinosaurs, a so-called "Escape the Room" dinosaur adventure, a 4D movie about dinosaurs and, among other things, a giant dinosaur Ferris wheel, together with several other attractions that play with the dinosaur theme. You do not even have to be interested in dinosaurs to find it exciting and fun!

Directions: The easiest way to get to Dinosaur Planet is by skytrain. Just get off at Phrom Phong Station on the Sukhumvit Line. The park is located right next to the adjacent shopping mall The Emporium.
Opening hours: Daily 10.00 - 22.00 (to get the most out of a visit, it is recommended to arrive sometime after 18.00).
Admission fees: Adults 600 baht. Children 400 baht. Free admission for children under 90 cm.

Dream World

Just outside Bangkok's northern boundaries lies the suburb Rangsit, where you will find Dream World. This is an amusement park with many faces. On the one hand, you have the large funfair with merry-go-rounds, roller coasters, haunted houses, and log flumes. On the other hand, there is the water park with a playground utterly drenched by spouting fountains.

What makes Dream World special is that the amusement park and the water park have also been combined with a really entertaining mini zoo called the Animal Farm. Here you can get really close to the animals and enjoy fun-filled shows with healthy and well-trained cats, dogs, and horses. And do not miss the opportunity to step into the giant birdcage to feed the birds; myriads of parrots that are more likely to be interested in pinching people's ears than feeding on the snacks offered.

In the park, there is also a 4D movie theater, in addition to several exciting shows. One of the more spectacular is Hollywood Action. In this show, the audience is invited to take part in the re-enactment of a live action movie. You can expect loud explosions, death defying stunts, fistfights, and everything else that comprises the makeup of an action-packed blockbuster.

Dream World can also boast having the first real Snow Town in Thailand. In the middle of the park, a sub-zero landscape with actual snow has been constructed, with an average temperature of 4 degrees below zero. Warm clothes and sledges are included in the admission fee.

Directions: The easiest way to get to Dream World is by taxi. To shorten the taxi ride, you could go by skytrain to the end station Mor Chit on the Sukhumvit Line, or by subway to the station Phahon Yothin or Lat Phrao, and from there continue by tuk-tuk or taxi.

Opening hours: Daily 10.00 – 17.00. Extended opening hours on national holidays.

Admission fees: Adults and children 550 baht. Free admission for children under 90 cm. The ticket includes most rides and activities, with the exception of Snow Town, Animal Farm, and the Water Park.

Dusit Zoo

Visiting a zoo in Asia might be an unpleasant and somewhat depressing experience. Animals in too small and dirty cages, inappropriate environments, uneducated staff, and too big of a focus on entertainment are some of the issues one might encounter. This, however, is not the case with Bangkok's largest zoo Dusit Zoo, which is under both state administration and Royal Protection. The park is of a high standard and all the animals are healthy and well-fed.

Dusit Zoo offers a wide range of animal shows, for example, the Seal Show, where the audience is treated to many laughs and eye-catching tricks. Other fun and interesting activities include feeding barnyard animals and fishing for small sharks, but without any dangerous hooks. The rather vast area for sea living creatures and reptiles, spiders and snakes is also of a very high standard, offering a wide variety of both informative and entertaining displays.

At Dusit Zoo, you can hire bicycles to get around. There are also pedal boats available, in which you can explore the artificial lake in the middle of the park. This lake is filled to the brim with giant monitor lizards, huge carps, and impressive turtles which you can feed from the boat. A visit to Dusit Zoo is most fun during the weekend as there are more things to do then, and more shows to watch.

Directions: The easiest way to get to Dusit Zoo is by taxi or tuk-tuk. To shorten the taxi ride, you could go by skytrain to the station Phayatai on the Sukhumvit Line, and there flag down a tuk-tuk or taxi to continue to Dusit Zoo.
Opening hours: Daily 08.00 – 18.00.
Admission fees: Adults 100 baht. Children 50 baht.

Escape Rooms Bangkok

A relatively new addition to Bangkok's many tourist attractions are the three big "Escape the Room" adventures. This concept can be found in many countries around the world, and most of the establishments in Bangkok are franchises of international companies with a professional approach and a high standard.

The aim of the game is to solve clues and unravel mysteries or committed crimes in locked rooms. The rooms come in many different forms and styles. Some have a horror theme, others are constructed like classic murder mystery plots, and a few take place in the future. You do not have to worry about getting stuck on any of the clues since all the rooms are monitored, allowing the players to call for help, if necessary. You can also choose between various degrees of difficulty. The level of excitement is extremely high, and without teamwork you will get stuck. All of the rooms are fairly similar in concept, with the big exception of Escape Room Bangkok, where there is a horror theme that might be inappropriate for younger children. The recommended minimum age is 7 years old.

All Escape Rooms are located in well-known shopping centers, which can turn the trip into a whole day event. Especially if you are visiting Escape Room Bangkok, as it is in one of Thailand's most famous budget shopping malls, namely MBK.

Directions: The Escape Hunt Experience is located right outside Asok skytrain station on the Sukhumvit Line, exit 6 towards Interchange 21 Tower Building. You can also get off at the subway station Sukhumvit. Ticket to Mystery is located in the shopping center Gateway Ekkamai, which lies right next to the skytrain station Ekkamai on the Sukhumvit Line. Escape Room Bangkok is located in the shopping center MBK, close to the central skytrain station Siam, as well as adjacent to the skytrain station National Stadium on the Silom Line.

Opening hours: The Escape Hunt Experience daily 10.00 – 19.00. Escape Room Bangkok daily 10.15 – 21.30. Ticket to Mystery daily 10.30 – 21.00.

Admission fees: The Escape Hunt Experience 900 baht per player. Escape Room Bangkok 550 baht per player. Ticket to Mystery 800 baht per player.

Fantasia Lagoon/Paradise Water Park

The heat in Bangkok can at times be intense, and what better way to escape it than a trip to a swimming pool. Fantasia Lagoon, also known as Paradise Water Park, is a fun-filled water park located on the rooftop of the shopping center The Mall Bangkae. In addition, this water park is much closer to central Bangkok than, for example, the more well-known water park of Suan Siam, as well as to a much lower price. The admission fee is only 100 baht, and for this very moderate sum you get access to a huge water park divided into several age-appropriate play zones: Fantasy Fountain for the youngest, Pirate Cove and The Slider Tower for the more adventurous, and Magic Jungle, Mystery Island and Ocean 10 for everyone else.

Occasionally, there are entertaining magic shows for the kids, most often on weekends and national holidays. Besides the pools, you will find many small restaurants and ice-cream parlors in the area. Since Fantasia Lagoon is situated on the rooftop of a shopping mall, there are plenty of opportunities to enjoy yourself in the gaming arcade on the floor right beneath the swimming pools. Here they have constructed a kind of Cartoon Town with houses and playgrounds built in the style of colorful cartoons, topped off with a vaulted roof painted as a bright summer's day, along with a small indoor waterfall.

Directions: The easiest was to get to The Mall Bangkae/Fantasia Lagoon in the outskirts of western Bangkok is by taxi. You can also go by skytrain to the end station Bangwa on the Silom Line, and from there continue in a tuk-tuk or taxi.
Opening hours: Monday to Friday 10.30 – 22.00. Saturday and Sunday 10.00 – 22.00. Fantasia Lagoon closes approximately one hour before the rest of the shopping mall.
Admission fees: 100 baht for adults and children over 100 cm. Free admission for children under 100 cm. Giant inflatable swim rings for 40 baht. Towels can be rented.

Fishing

The last thing you might think of when visiting Bangkok is going fishing. Nonetheless, there are several big artificial lakes just outside central Bangkok, most of which have a wide selection of some of the largest freshwater fish in the world, including species that can weigh as much as 100 kg.

The nicest and, not least, most modern fishing park in Bangkok is Bungsamran Fishing Park. At Bungsamran, you can fish 24 hours a day. In addition, there are bungalows to rent if you are interested in night fishing. The bungalows are situated right next to the lake, and you can sit and fish from your own porch, which stretches out into the water. You do not have to bring your own equipment, as everything can either be rented or bought at the park.

Several International Game Fish Association (IGFA) records have been set at Bungsamran, and it is considered to be one of the best spots in the whole of Thailand. However, you do not need to be a professional fisherman to fish here, or even an adult, since the lake is divided into sections with fish of various sizes. As long as you are old enough to handle a rod, you will have a great time at Bungsamran.

Directions: The easiest way to get to Bungsamran Fishing Park, which is located in the northeast of greater Bangkok, is by taxi. For your convenience, show the driver the map that can be found on Bungsamran's website. Alternatively, let the driver speak to someone in the staff at Bungsamran.
Opening hours: 24 hours a day.
Fees: Fishing 600 – 2 000 baht. Accompanying fishing guide 1 000 baht. Bungalows and hotel rooms 600 – 4 000 baht, depending on standard and size.

Flow House Bangkok

In the middle of Bangkok, you will find one of the most unique ways to cool down from the at times scorching heat, namely Flow House Bangkok. At Flow House Bangkok, you can choose to surf with either a body board or a surfboard on real waves created in a sloping pool powered by a state-of-the-art FlowRider machine. The equipment has been imported from San Diego, USA, and is available at just a few places in Thailand.

Flow House Bangkok is open to everyone between 5 and 100 years old. Besides surfing, at the Flow House you can also play pool, darts, and ping pong, as well as enjoying two large golf simulators. The management has, in addition, constructed a small putting range adjacent to the game zone. In the restaurant, you will find a classic California inspired kitchen, with dishes like homemade pizzas, BBQ burgers, and all kinds of hot dogs.

You can either book a surf spot at the location or, preferably, via their website. The surf sessions kick off on the hour, every hour, and you should have arrived about 30 minutes before your booking is due to start.

Directions: The easiest way to get to Flow House Bangkok is by skytrain. Get off at Phrom Phong Station on the Sukhumvit Line and leave by exit 6. Walk down Sukhumvit soi 26, pass the big hotel The Davis Bangkok. To your left at the following three-way intersection, right before McDonald's, you will see a sign pointing you in the right direction.
Opening hours: Monday to Friday 14.00 – 23.00. Saturday and Sunday 10.00 – 23.00.
Fees: Surfing starts at 550 baht per hour. Quantity discounts are offered.

Funarium

The Funarium is one of Bangkok's largest indoor playgrounds. The target group are children up to the age of 12. For the younger kids in the family, there are safe play areas with slides, huge ball pits, sandboxes, and small spouting fountains. For the older kids, there are climbing walls, large slides, a two-story high playhouse, and massive trampolines. Moreover, you can borrow bicycles and roller blades to go for a ride on the indoor tracks. There is also the option of playing football or basketball in the area. In addition to the play zones, the management has constructed a small arts and crafts center where the children have access to a wide range of materials. Another fun activity, for the somewhat older children, are the cooking courses that usually are available during weekends.

The Funarium is popular among both Thai families and expat families living in Bangkok, and while the children are playing the adults can relax in the massage parlor next door.

Directions: The easiest way to get to the Funarium is by taxi or skytrain. The Funarium is located at soi Attakravi, next to the small shopping mall Big C, which lies a stone's throw from Sukhumvit soi 26 and Rama 4 Road. It is, however, a bit tucked away, and you are advised to check the Funarium's website for a more detailed map.
Opening hours: Monday to Thursday 09.00 – 18.00. Friday to Sunday 09.00 – 19.00.
Admission fees: 200 baht for 3 hours for children under 105 cm. 320 baht for 3 hours for children over 105 cm. Adults (over 13 years old) 110 baht.

Harbin Ice Wonderland

Lately, several so-called Snow Towns have popped up in Bangkok. One of the newest, and definitely biggest, which opened in 2014, is Harbin Ice Wonderland. Unlike other Snow Towns in and around Bangkok, Harbin Ice Wonderland is not a small part of a larger destination, but rather the main attraction itself. Warm clothes, ice skates, and sledges are rented out by the hour.

Besides play grounds, icy slopes and skating rinks, this very cold Snow Town has been decorated with sculptures made out of ice depicting famous landmarks around the world, such as the Eiffel tower in Paris and the Big Ben in London. Moreover, there is a bar for the adults where everything, including the actual drinking-glasses, has been carved out of ice.

Directions: The easiest way to get to Harbin Ice Wonderland is by skytrain. Get off at Bearing on the Sukhumvit Line and leave the station in the opposite direction of the train. Harbin Ice Wonderland is within walking distance of the exit.

Opening hours: Daily 10.00 – 19.00. *Harbin Ice Wonderland has undergone renovations lately and it is advisable to consult their website or Facebook page before going to see if they have reopened yet.*

Admission fees: Adults and children 550 baht.

Imaginia Playland & Benjasiri Park

Imaginia Playland is the newest, most innovative and creative playland in Bangkok. It is not only about swings, bouncy castles, playgrounds, and slides, but also about arts and crafts, music, theater and, not least, books and reading. Moreover, there is an actual farm, right next to the playland, which has been built in order to let the inner-city kids of Bangkok see, meet, touch, and learn about real animals.

Imaginia Playland, as well as the farm EM Farm, is part of the exclusive shopping mall The Emporium. As an added bonus, The Emporium lies next to Benjasiri Park, which many regard as being the nicest park in Bangkok. It is smaller than the more well-known park of Lumpini, but because of that also much easier to get around in. There is always something fun going on at Benjasiri, especially after the sweltering sun has set, as the park has become a meeting place for culture events and fitness activities. There are also several big playgrounds in the park, as well as a daily Musical Fountain Show.

Directions: The easiest way to get to Imaginia Playland and The Emporium is by skytrain. The Emporium lies adjacent to the station Phrom Phong on the Sukhumvit Line, and Benjasiri Park is just a stone's throw from The Emporium.

Opening hours: Imaginia Playland daily 10.00 – 20.00. The Emporium daily 10.00 – 22.00.

Admission fees: 100 baht for children under 70 cm. 250 baht for children 71 – 90 cm. 480 baht for children over 91 cm. 200 baht for adults (over 15 years old).

Ice-skating

There are several big skating rinks in Bangkok, and four of the best are located in, or close to, Bangkok's downtown. The perhaps nicest is in Siam Discovery Center, which you can reach from one of the exits at the skytrain station Siam. If getting off at Siam, you are also close to the other large skating rink in central Bangkok, namely the one at Central World. At the subway station Phra Ram 9 lies the shopping mall Central Plaza, which is a branch of Central World, where you will find the third skating rink. In the same area, you also have access to the fourth skating rink, which is located in the competing shopping mall The Esplanade.

Ice-skating can, in all the various rinks, be combined with other fun activities and excursions. For example, Art in Paradise is in The Esplanade, and around the skytrain station Siam you will find, among other things, Sea Life Bangkok Ocean World and Madame Tussauds.

Directions: The easiest way to get to the various skating rinks is by skytrain or subway. For ice-skating at Central World and Siam Discovery Center, get off the skytrain at Siam. For ice-skating at Central Plaza, get off the subway at Phra Ram 9. For ice-skating at The Esplanade, get off the subway at Thailand Cultural Center.
Opening hours: Daily 10.00 – 21.00.
Fees: Ice-skating starts at 100 baht per person (the equipment is included in the price). For a small additional fee, you can take ice-skating lessons at all the abovementioned locations.

KidZania

A somewhat different excursion for the kids in Bangkok is a visit to KidZania in Paragon Shopping Center. KidZania is a miniature city on a rather grand scale. What makes the city of KidZania so unique is the fact that the children do not only play here, but actually try out all sorts of different occupations. In the city of KidZania, there is a multitude of jobs to choose between, and all of them have been constructed according to real life situations. The children are allowed to do everything that adults do in their respective job roles, and they also earn so-called KidZania dollars from the work they put in. This money can then be used in a shop in the play city.

KidZania is relatively new and very elaborate. For the children it feels like "real work", especially when they get the opportunity to dress up like an actual pilot or perhaps doctor. Children that enter KidZania by themselves need to have some basic English skills to be able to understand the instructions. Younger children are welcome to participate in the company of an adult. There is also a small café in KidZania where parents can relax over a cup of coffee or tea while the kids explore the city.

The main target group are children between the ages of 4 and 14. If a child chooses to enter by himself or herself, the parents are required to leave a phone number where they can be contacted in case of an emergency. There are also routines in place for leaving KidZania so that no child wanders off by mistake. A visit to KidZania usually lasts for at least 3 to 4 hours, since there is so much to do, and so many jobs to try out.

Directions: The easiest way to get to KidZania is by skytrain. Get off at the central station Siam and follow the signs to Paragon Shopping Center. KidZania is on the 5th floor.
Opening hours: Monday to Friday 10.00 – 17.00. Saturday and Sunday 10.30 – 20.30.
Admission fees: Monday to Friday 425 baht for adults and children 2 – 3 years old, and 825 baht for children 4 – 14 years old. Saturday and Sunday 500 baht for adults and children 2 – 3 years old, and 1 000 baht for children 4 – 14 years old. Free admission for all children under the age of 2.

Asia Revealed Publishing Company

Leoland Water Park & Mega Bangna

If you would like to combine go-carts with swimming, then a trip to the shopping mall Central Plaza Bangna is something for you. Here you will find a huge water park with both fast and big slides, all sorts of different kinds of swimming pools, and plenty of room for sunbathing and relaxing. Moreover, there is not only a go-cart track right next to the water park, but also a gaming arcade, along with a small funfair.

As with many other playlands and water parks in Bangkok, Leoland Water Park is located inside a shopping center. As an added bonus, Central Plaza Bangna and Leoland Water Park are only a couple of kilometers from the brand-new shopping mall Mega Bangna, which can boast a state-of-the-art skating rink, an enormous bowling alley, and a super-modern cinema complex. Moreover, Mega Bangna is the first, and so far the only, shopping mall with a full-scale IKEA.

Directions: The easiest way to get to Leoland Water Park is by taxi. Tell the driver to stop at Central Plaza Bangna. You could also travel by skytrain to Bang Na on the Sukhumvit Line, and then walk for approximately 5 to 10 minutes along the Bangna-Trat Road. If you instead want to go to Mega Bangna, the easiest way is to take the skytrain to Udomsak on the Sukhumvit Line and then, from the street outside, catch the free shuttlebus to the shopping mall.
Opening hours Leoland Water Park: Monday to Friday 11.00 – 18.00. Saturday and Sunday 10.00 – 19.00.
Admission fees: Adults and children 100 baht per person. Additional fees for go-carts and rides at the amusement park.

Lumpini Park

The well-known park of Lumpini lies smack in the middle of Bangkok and offers a nice alternative to the usual big city attractions. The park is typically empty during the day due to the heat, but in the evening, it literally explodes with people and activities.

Lumpini has among the Bangkokians become synonymous with health and exercise. In the huge park, there is a three-kilometer-long jogging trail, where an additional lane for bicycles has been constructed. You will also find a big outdoor gym in the park, which only costs a few baht to use, as well as a large number of public fitness machines laid out among the lawns in the form of a training track. In addition, there is a large swimming pool, which, however, requires a membership. This membership can, nonetheless, be sorted out quickly on the spot for an extremely low fee.

The most entertaining workout option is, though, the big aerobic sessions that spring up all around the park after sunset. Mobile scenes and sound systems are erected and professional trainers hold dance inspired workout sessions for anyone who wishes to join. The children, on the other hand, can enjoy themselves at one of the many big playgrounds. To top it off, a large artificial lake is located in the middle of the park, filled to the brim with giant lizards, huge carps, and various turtles. Pedal boats for rent are available.

Directions: The easiest way to get to Lumpini Park is by skytrain or subway. If going by skytrain, get off at Sala Daeng on the Silom Line. If going by subway, get off at Silom or Lumpini.
Opening hours: Daily 04.30 – 21.00.
Admission fees: Free admission for all.

Madame Tussauds

In Bangkok's downtown, which is centered around the skytrain station Siam, lies Madame Tussauds. Since this Madame Tussauds is a branch of Madame Tussauds in London, all the wax figures are of a standard that equals the ones in England. The figures are divided into nine categories, 1) Red Carpet Zone, 2) Music Zone, 3) History Zone, 4) Film Zone, 5) Leaders Zone, 6) Authentic History Zone, 7) Art & Science Zone, 8) TV Zone, and 9) Sports Zone. There are a couple of Asian stars in each category at Madame Tussauds Bangkok that could be unfamiliar to visitors from other parts of the world. Most of the figures, though, depict internationally famous men and women.

In addition, there are several interactive games at the location. You can, for example, play golf against Tiger Woods, or test your IQ against Albert Einstein. Due to the close proximity to the shopping center Paragon, visitors to Madame Tussauds have the opportunity to buy tickets to Sea Life Bangkok Ocean World at a greatly reduced price. Together, these two excursions take up most of the day. There are, however, plenty of restaurants and cafés scattered around the shopping malls where you can relax between the visits.

Directions: The easiest way to get to Madame Tussauds is by skytrain. Get off at the central station Siam and follow the signs to the shopping center Siam Discovery.
Opening hours: Daily 10.00 – 21.00.
Admission fees: 850 baht for adults and children over the age of 11, and 650 baht for children between 3 and 10 years old. Free admission for children under the age of 3.

Safari World

Safari World is, like many other big entertainment venues in and outside Bangkok, a combination of several different kinds of parks. The main attraction is, nonetheless, an 8-kilometer-long tour through the safari park in either your own vehicle or in a shared pickup. During this trip, you will get the opportunity to see one of few feeding shows of lions and tigers in the world. In addition, English speaking guides join every trip.

Besides the safari tour, there is Marine World, where you can enjoy entertaining shows featuring dolphins and sea lions, among other animals. In an adjacent part of the park, River Safari World, you can ride log flumes through landscapes representing the jungles of Asia and Africa. In another section of Safari World, there is a long walking trail, along several large animal enclosures, which connects to a giant birdcage where the visitors are allowed to feed the exotic birds. When visiting Safari World, you will also have the chance to go and see several entertaining stunt and cowboy shows.

Directions: The easiest way to get to Safari World, in the northeast of greater Bangkok, is by taxi. The bus routes 60, 71, and 501 stop, however, at the nearby shopping mall Fashion Island, and from there you can continue in a tuk-tuk or taxi.
Opening hours: Monday to Friday 09.00 – 16.30. Saturday and Sunday 09.00 – 17.00.
Admission fees for adults: Only Safari World 800 baht. Only Marine Park 1 000 baht. Combination ticket for Safari World and Marine Park 1 200 baht. Combination ticket with buffet lunch 1 550 baht. Only River Safari Ride 350 baht.
Admission fees for children (under 140 cm): Only Safari World 700 baht. Only Marine Park 800 baht. Combination ticket for Safari World and Marine Park 900 baht. Combination ticket with buffet lunch 1 200 baht. Only River Safari Ride 350 baht. Free admission for children under 100 cm.

Samut Prakarn Crocodile Farm and Zoo

In the outskirts of southern Bangkok lies one of the world's largest crocodile farms, where, at least according to the management of the zoo, the world's biggest crocodile lives. Visitors to the park can enjoy various crocodile shows with experienced trainers who, among other stunts, stick their heads into the jaws of the crocodiles. You can also try out feeding the crocodiles yourself – but, of course, from a safe distance. In addition to the crocodiles, the management has brought in several other animals, including elephants, which means that shorter elephant rides are available. There are also shows with monkeys and camels to enjoy, as well as a somewhat quirky dinosaur museum.

The park is really big and it includes a small lake with pedal boats for hire. Unlike Dusit Zoo, the focus of Samut Prakarn Crocodile Farm and Zoo is mainly on entertainment, which means that some visitors might find the whole thing a bit unpleasant. Nonetheless, the park does, to some extent, take part in the research, and preservation, of crocodiles.

Directions: The easiest way to get to Samut Prakarn Crocodile Farm and Zoo is by taxi. You can also go by skytrain to the end station Bearing on the Sukhumvit Line, and from there continue in a tuk-tuk or taxi.
Opening hours: Daily 08.00 – 18.00.
Admission fees: Adults 300 baht. Children 200 baht.

Sea Life Bangkok Ocean World

On the ground floor of the huge shopping mall Paragon lies Sea Life Bangkok Ocean World, which is the biggest aquarium in the whole of Southeast Asia. Sea Life Bangkok Ocean World is the home of sea creatures ranging from the absolute smallest to some of the largest and most striking. Penguins, sting rays, sharks, and enormous freshwater fish can be observed through gigantic window walls offering panoramic views over lifelike underwater environments.

The most impressive part of the aquarium is, however, the long glass tunnel which is laid out below the bigger tanks of sea creatures. In some of the smaller tanks, you will find animals that are not as dangerous, but oh so much more terrifying, such as the enormous spider crab, the giant squid, and the fluorescent jellyfish. Several other activities are offered at Sea Life Bangkok Ocean World to make the visit more fun and exciting. You can, for example, feed the animals from a small boat, which is visible to the guests walking through the glass tunnel underneath it. Moreover, there is the option of renting a specially designed diving suit for walks on the seabed to get really close to the stingrays and sharks. The newest addition to Sea Life Bangkok Ocean World is a 4D cinema. On the premises, you will also find a large playground for the younger kids in the family.

A trip to Sea Life Bangkok Ocean World can easily be combined with other fun activities in the area as it is located in downtown Siam.

Directions: The easiest way to get to Sea Life Bangkok Ocean World is by skytrain. Get off at the central station Siam and follow the signs to the shopping center Paragon.
Opening hours: Daily 10.00 – 21.00. Last entry at 20.00.
Admission fees: Adults 900 baht. Children 500 baht. 4D cinema 250 baht. Feeding sharks 180 baht. Sea walk with diving suit 2 000 baht. Diving/swimming with the sharks 5 000 to 7 000 baht, depending on prior experience.

Siam Niramit Show

One of the biggest shows in the world is Siam Niramit, which can be found in both Bangkok and Phuket. Over one hundred actors, changing costumes up to five hundred times, take part in the show. The show itself is about Thailand and comes in three acts. In act one, the audience is informed about the four geographical areas that Thailand has been divided into and how they have evolved during the last 700 years. In act two, Thai belief systems, myths, and folklores are enacted. In act three, all the different customs and festivals which make up the core of what one might call *"Thainess"* is brought to life on stage. However, this is not your normal theater production, but rather a grand spectacle with impressive special effects and extravagant props.

A couple of hours before the start of every show, the audience is invited to try out, and take part in, various local customs, such as playing classical instruments, make batik, and bake delicacies.

Directions: The easiest way to get to Siam Niramit is by subway. Get off at Thailand Cultural Center. Outside exit 1, there are free shuttle buses departing daily between 18.00 and 19.45.

Opening hours: Daily 20.00. The show lasts for about 80 minutes. Additional activities on the premises start at 17.00.
Admission fees: Only the show 1500 – 2000 baht. Show and dinner 1720 – 2350 baht. Tickets are preferably booked on the website of Siam Niramit.

Snake Farm

The Snake Farm in Bangkok, managed by the Red Cross, is an important part in the research of snakes, as well as in the production of antivenin. The area is divided into an indoor and outdoor section. In the indoor section, visitors can learn about snakes in general, in addition to what you should do in case of being bitten. Here you will find a variety of displays with interactive functions about snakes and their habitats. Moreover, the visitors are also invited to experience the process of extracting poison from the snakes used for producing antivenin.

In the outdoor section, there is a zoo with snakes from many different geographical areas of Southeast Asia. It is also in this section that the daily snake show takes place. The staff displays and informs about a number of venomous and non-venomous snakes in the form of an exciting show, which is ended with the audience being allowed to hold some of the really large specimens, such as the enormous anaconda. There will be plenty of photo opportunities; however, not from a distance, but with the snakes hanging over and around one's neck and shoulders.

Directions: The easiest way to get to the Snake Farm is by taxi or tuk-tuk. The Snake Farm is, nonetheless, located within walking distance of the skytrain station Sala Daeng on the Silom Line. Leave the station via exit 3 or 4 and head towards Rama 4 Road and Henry Dunang Road. Within 200 meters, there are signs on your right side to the Snake Farm and the Red Cross.
Opening hours: Monday to Friday 08.30 – 16.00. Saturday and Sunday 09.30 – 13.00. Visit the Snake Farm's website to see when the daily shows start.

Admission fees: Adults 200 baht. Children 50 baht.

Snow Town & Kidzoona

One of the biggest, and nicest, snow towns of Southeast Asia is located in the shopping center Gateway Ekkamai. The area occupies the greater part of an entire floor and is constructed in the guise of a small Japanese country town. There are a couple of restaurants and shops in the little town, in addition to a 30-centimeter-deep blanket of snow to play in. Furthermore, a small ski slope has been built, where the visitors not only can go skiing, but also take skiing lessons.

Inside the shopping mall of Gateway Ekkamai, there is a huge play zone called Kidzoona and Molly Fantasy, which is divided into various areas reserved for all sorts of different games and activities. It is bright, colorful, and really fun. Here you will find everything from giant inflatable slides to big ball pits and small merry-go-rounds. The age groups targeted are from the very youngest up to a maximum age of 12. Trained staff is on duty at all times. In addition, there is a gaming arcade right next to Kidzoona and Molly Fantasy, where the teenagers of the family can enjoy themselves while the younger children are playing.

Directions: The easiest way to get to Gateway Ekkamai is by skytrain. The shopping mall lies adjacent to the station Ekkamai on the Sukhumvit Line.
Opening hours Snow Town: Monday to Friday 11.00 – 22.00. Saturday and Sunday 10.00 – 22.00.
Opening hours Kidzoona and Molly Fantasy: Daily 10.00 – 21.00.
Admission fees for Snow Town: Adults (over 90 cm) 100 baht. Children (under 90 cm) 80 baht. A small fee is charged for renting warm clothes and skis.
Admission fees for Kidzoona and Molly Fantasy: Children 180 baht. Adults 90 baht.

Suan Siam Water Park/Siam Park City

In the northern outskirts of Bangkok lies the water and amusement park Siam Park City, also called Suan Siam Water Park. This really large park is divided into five zones – Water Park, X-Zone, Family World, Fantasy World, and Small World – targeting different age groups. For the teenagers and adults there are, among other things, log flumes and roller coasters of a high international standard, and for the younger kids a wide array of merry-go-rounds, rides, and games. It does not matter how old or young you are since everyone can find something exciting to do at Siam Park City.

About a third of the park is occupied by the Water Park. The Water Park itself is divided into many smaller areas centered around a big pool with a wave machine. Many of the smaller pools are connected to the waterslides in the area. Moreover, there is a several meter wide canal running through the zone and in which you can slowly and leisurely drift along the weak currents on huge swim rings. You do not have to visit both the Water Park and the Amusement Park at the same time, as you have the option of only buying tickets for the zones that you and your family wish to use, which could save you a lot of money if visiting the park with really young children.

Directions: The easiest way to get to Suan Siam Water Park is by taxi. Alternatively, you can get off the skytrain at the end station Mor Chit on the Sukhumvit Line, and from there continue in a tuk-tuk or taxi.
Opening hours: Daily 10.00 – 18.00.
Admission fees: All-inclusive tickets for adults 900 baht. All-inclusive tickets for children 700 baht. If visiting with children under 130 cm, it is recommended to buy tickets for each respective zone.

Wakeboarding

When visiting Bangkok, you will not only find a multitude of big city attractions, but also several exhilarating nature activities. One of these is Thai

Wake Park. Wakeboarding is a kind of water-skiing; however, you do not use water skis, but rather a kind of snowboard, and the speedboat is replaced by an elevated cable system pulling you along the lake. The cable system comes with courses for both absolute beginners and professionals. Although no previous experience is required, wakeboarding might be a bit too physically demanding for the younger members of the family.

At Thai Wake Park they have, however, done their best to make sure that everyone will have an enjoyable experience. There is, for example, a manmade little island in the middle of the lake making sure that the wind does not create any unnecessary ripples. In addition, if you fall the staff will rush to your aid in a boat, enabling you to quickly reconnect to the cable system and continue surfing. At the premises, there is also a hotel offering substantial discounts for wakeboarding customers.

Directions: The easiest way to get to Thai Wake Park is by taxi. For your convenience, show the driver the map that can be found on their website. Alternatively, let the driver speak to someone in the staff at Thai Wake Park.
Opening hours: From morning to night all year round.
Fees: 2 hours for 850 baht. 4 hours for 1 150 baht. All day for 1 350 baht. Wakeboarding at night: standard fees plus a surcharge of 100 baht. Additional fees might apply for renting the equipment.

Yoyo Land

At Seacon Square in the east of Bangkok, there is a huge entertainment center for kids called Yoyo Land. The play area is truly massive for being located indoors, and here you will be able to let the kids enjoy themselves fully by visiting the funfair, get creative in the arts and crafts center, play games in the arcade, watch movies at the cinema, go for a ride on a miniature train, dive in the ball pits, or explore the adventure zone with all its thrilling stations. Moreover, the management has also created a mini-version of KidZania. This one is, however, incorporated into the play area and can be completed a lot quicker, and to a much lower price.

The target group of Yoyo Land are children between the ages of 3 and 11. However, slightly older children will probably also find it fun, especially since Yoyo Land is located in a large shopping mall.

Directions: The easiest way to get to Seacon Square is by taxi. Alternatively, you can get off the skytrain at the stations On Nut or Udomsak on the Sukhumvit Line, and from there continue in a tuk-tuk or taxi.

Opening hours: Monday to Friday 11.00 – 18.00. Saturday and Sunday 11.00 – 19.30.

Admission fees: Free admission. However, the activities cost 10 – 150 baht per person.

Chiang Mai

Among the mountain ranges of northern Thailand, approximately 700 kilometers from Bangkok, lies the city of Chiang Mai. This provincial capital has roots stretching almost a thousand years back in time, and used to be the center of the former kingdom of Lanna. Chiang Mai's importance arose from its location at the river Ping and this, eventually, led to the establishment of some major trading routes between India in the west and China in the northeast.

In today's Thailand, Chiang Mai has evolved into one of the most visited cities in the entire country. However, the influx of tourists does not only constitute of foreigners; domestic tourists also flock in droves to Chiang Mai. Mainly because of the weather, which, during most of the year, is somewhat cooler than in many other parts of Thailand.

When arriving to Chiang Mai, the first thing that strikes you is how majestic the nature is, as well as the stark difference between the ecosystem of the north and the golden beaches of the south. Chiang Mai is surrounded by thick jungles along with high mountains and the hilly, undulating vegetation blanketing the area seems to have been colored in with bright crayons. In contrast to Bangkok, here you want to spend as much time as possible outdoors, as the landscape is made for adventure activities.

There is a wide range of excursions and attractions offered in and around Chiang Mai that will suit everyone in the family, regardless of interests, such as exploring caves, trekking on ATVs and motorcycles, swimming in waterfalls, and ziplining through the high canopies.

Art in Paradise

Art in Paradise Chiang Mai is, as the main branch in Bangkok, a gallery with interactive 3D paintings; however, not in the form of holograms, but in the guise of actual paintings. What it is about is creating the illusion of the beholder stepping into the artwork. The paintings are huge, sometimes covering entire walls, and offer amazing photo opportunities where oneself, so to say, becomes part of the motif. Next to most of the paintings, there are instructions on how you should position yourself to best create the impression of being an integral part of the composition.

The optical illusions are spectacular and the whole family will be fascinated by the end result when captured by your own camera. You could say that all the paintings at Art in Paradise are incomplete until someone actually steps into them. In addition, there is a nice café and a restaurant on the premises where you can enjoy a snack or a full dinner after or before your visit.

Directions: The easiest way to get to Art in Paradise is on foot, or by some kind of taxi. The gallery is located in central Chiang Mai, just a couple of hundred meters south of Shangri-La Hotel on Chang Klan Road.
Opening hours: Daily 09.00 – 21.00.
Admission fees: Adults 400 baht. Children 200 baht. Free admission for children under 100 cm.

Caves and Caving

Chiang Mai is surrounded by mountains and thick jungles, making it ideal for not only treks and swimming trips to beautiful waterfalls, but also for caving in fascinating environments. In Chiang Mai, you will find some of Thailand's most famous cave systems, completed with long tunnels, winding staircases cut out from the bedrock, narrow pathways, and grand halls with stunningly decorated temples.

Muang On Cave

Muang on Cave does not belong to the category of really big cave systems; however, it is big enough for the adventurous family, as well as highly interesting. This system consists largely of big hallways and rooms in the mountain decorated and fitted out with enormous Buddha statues and small shrines. The pathways are lit and the walk relatively comfortable, meaning that even rather young children can navigate the corridors of the mountain.

Right outside the caves are a couple of restaurants where you can relax before or after the excursion. Other fun tourist attractions can, in addition, be found close by, for example, San Kamphaeng Hot Springs.

Chiang Dao Caves

A much larger cave system, which lies a bit further away from Chiang Mai, is Chiang Dao Caves. It is, on the other hand, much more thrilling to explore. This system consists of more than 100 caves; however, only five are open to the public. You gain access to them by first entering the main cave, where you need to stop at a station manned by trained guides. From this point, you can access all five systems. Two of them are lit and most people, regardless of age, should be able to explore them relatively effortlessly. The remaining three, though, are nestled into the mountain in complete darkness. You can either rent a lantern at the station and investigate them by yourself, or pay for a guide to join you. The cost is low, only 100 baht, which is for the lantern. The guide's only wage will be the tip from the guests.

Since these caves are at times narrow, slippery, and somewhat perilous, it is recommended to enter them in the company of a skilled guide, who, in addition, will be able to point out all the remarkable features of the caves that you otherwise might miss.

Directions: The easiest way to get to Muang On Cave is by your own vehicle, or some kind of taxi. Muang On Cave is located about 30 kilometers east of Chiang Mai along route 1317. The distance to Chiang Dao Caves is,

on the other hand, over 70 kilometers. The cave system is located north of Chiang Mai along route 107. There are, however, pickup taxis from Chiang Mai that pass Chiang Dao Caves, and which cost less than 100 baht.
Opening hours: Daily 07.00 – 17.00.
Admission fees for Muang On Cave: 30 baht.
Admission fees for Chiang Dao Caves: 40 baht. Rent a private guide with a lantern for 100 baht.

Central Festival: Ice-skating and Shopping

Central Festival is a shopping mall with branches all over Thailand. The branch in Chiang Mai can boast of having the city's only state-of-the-art skating rink, Sub-Zero Ice Skate Club, where you can also take skating lessons, if in need. There are plenty of good shopping opportunities at Central Festival, offering a wide range of both locally owned shops and huge international chains selling brand name goods. Other fun options at the mall include going bowling in a highly modern bowling alley, enjoying blockbusters at the cinema complex, or spending some time in the gaming arcade.

Central Festival is a convenient and relaxing big city alternative to the other mainly adventurous activities in and around Chiang Mai, most of which take place in the middle of the jungle or high up in the mountains.

Directions: The easiest way to get to Central Festival is on foot, or by some kind of taxi. The shopping mall is located in the northeast of central Chiang Mai.
Opening hours: Monday to Friday 11.00 – 21.00. Saturday and Sunday 10.00 – 22.00.
Admission fees: Ice-skating starts at 160 baht per hour. All day for 500 baht.

Chiang Mai X-Center

Just outside Chiang Mai lies the X-Center, offering a combination of adventure activities and motor sports. The selection of fun and exciting things to do is huge, as well as their range of vehicles: drifter go-carts, off-road buggies, motorcycles, and ATVs. The tracks are long, varied, and thrilling. There are trainers and coaches at the premises and you do not need to have any prior experience to be able to manage the tracks. For motorcycle enthusiasts, there is a bit more challenging option. Instead of riding premade tracks in the area, you can go jungle trekking on natural pathways and trails.

The adventure park also includes a paintball range, which is the biggest one in Chiang Mai. Furthermore, there is a Jungle Bungee Jump for everyone weighing over 35 kg, where you jump from a 50-meter-high tower towards a small lake. In addition, here you will find Zorb Balls, trampolines, playgrounds, and a small zipline course. The staff at the X-Center also arranges birthday parties with clowns and all sorts of other fun things for the kids.

Directions: The easiest way to get to Chiang Mai X-Center is by the park's own shuttle bus, free of charge from more or less any hotel in Chiang Mai. You could also get on one of Chiang Mai's many red pickup-taxis. If using your own vehicle, drive north from Chiang Mai via route 107. After approximately 20 kilometers, turn left on route 1096, and continue for another 10 kilometers. Chiang Mai X-Center is located in the same area as Mae Sa Snake Farm and Chiang Mai Monkey Center.
Opening hours: Daily from 09.00.
Fees: Off-road Buggies and ATVs range from 800 to 7 000 baht depending on engine size, activity, and length of time. Jungle Bungee Jump 2 000 baht. Drifter Go-Carts 800 baht. Paintball 300 baht. Off-road Trail Motorbike Tour starts at 2 500 baht. Zorb Balls 600 baht.

Chiang Mai Zoo & Aquarium

Chiang Mai Zoo & Aquarium is a large park that has been divided into two sections to which you can buy separate tickets.

Chiang Mai Zoo

Chiang Mai Zoo is of a high international standard. The park is spread out over a substantial plot of land compared to other zoos in Southeast Asia, and most of the animals have spacious cages or pens to move around in. Moreover, Chiang Mai Zoo is one of few zoos in the world that has been successful in breeding giant pandas. At Chiang Mai Zoo, the administration has also managed to successfully breed white tigers, and the staff at the zoo work continuously towards securing the future for several endangered species.

Some of the more common animals, for example, the seals and the birds, are on the other hand stars in a couple of fun-filled daily shows. Other local stars of the zoo include the koala bears, which the visitors are allowed to touch and take photos with under supervision. In the park, the staff has always at least one mini-zoo up and running for the younger members of the family, where they can cuddle and play with guinea pigs, rabbits, and other small animals.

On the premises of the huge park, you can either walk, jump on a minibus, or ride the monorail to get around. Another fun activity, especially during really hot days, is Chiang Mai Snow Dome, which is an indoor winter landscape with both snow and a small slope to ride sledges on. Every visit lasts for 30 minutes, and during this time you will be able to borrow both a sledge and warm clothes.

Chiang Mai Aquarium

When visiting the park, you will also find one of the biggest aquariums in the whole of Southeast Asia, which can boast of having one of the world's longest underwater tunnels made of glass, where the visitors, at the bottom of an artificial river and a sea, can observe sharks, sting rays, and huge freshwater fish. In addition, there are plenty of weird and wonderful sea creatures in the many smaller aquariums, for example, bizarre jellyfish, colorful seahorses, and giant squids. The more adventurous visitors are invited to dive in the aquariums to meet the stingrays and sharks at feeding time.

Several other fun activities are arranged just outside the aquarium. You can, for example, rent a pedal boat to feed the fish and turtles in the lake next to the aquarium, roll around in Zorb Balls, or go ziplining on a 200-meter-long course. A visit to the zoo and the aquarium will most definitely last all day, and it is recommended to come early in the morning.

Directions: The easiest way to get to Chiang Mai Zoo & Aquarium is by tuk-tuk or flagging down one of the red pickup-taxis. The Park is located just a couple of kilometers from the center of Chiang Mai.
Opening hours: Daily 08.00 – 18.00.
Admission fees for Chiang Mai Zoo: Adults 520 baht. Children (under 135 cm) 390 baht.
Admission fees for the Snow Dome: Adults 150 baht. Children 100 baht.

Doi Suthep

Young children and teenagers might not always be that fond of excursions to cultural places, but a visit to one of Thailand's most famous temples could well be worth it. The temple of Doi Suthep is located up in the mountains right outside Chiang Mai proper and offers, once you have climbed a long staircase that has been cut out of the mountain itself, a remarkable view of the surrounding area, as well as of the city of Chiang Mai. In addition, the premises are littered with interesting, thought-provoking, and remarkable statues and sculptures of varying sizes and forms.

In case you would not be able to conquer the stairs in the humid heat, there is a lift that will take you to the top for the meager sum of 30 baht. The actual temple area dates back to 1383, thus making it one of the oldest temples still in use in Thailand.

Directions: The easiest way to get to Doi Suthep is by your own vehicle, or some kind of taxi. The temple lies approximately 10 kilometers outside central Chiang Mai and can be seen from the city.
Opening hours: Daily 06.00 – 18.00.
Admission fees: Free admission for all.

Elephant Farms

In the vicinity of Chiang Mai, there are three large elephant farms, offering a wide range of activities and experiences.

Elephant Nature Park

At Elephant Nature Park, the focus is on rehabilitating abused and formerly captured elephants. No elephant riding is allowed but you can, on the other hand, participate in all the procedures put in place to reintroduce the elephants to their natural habitat, creating a much more intimate bond than that experienced when just going on a trek. Moreover, you are also allowed to be present when the elephants go about their own daily routines, for example, rummaging for food or bathing.

As a guest, you can book visits that last from a couple of hours to whole weeks, in addition to volunteering to work and live in the park, which, though, has an age limit of 18 years old. On the premises, there is also a home for abandoned and abused cats, dogs, birds, and water buffalos, among other animals.

Directions: The easiest way to get to Elephant Nature Park is by your own vehicle, or some kind of taxi. The park lies approximately 60 kilometers north of Chiang Mai. Leave the city via route 107, and then turn right after the intersection at route 3038.
Opening hours: All year round depending on booking arrangements.
Fees: The cost starts at around 2 500 baht for a whole day to 15 000 baht for weekly volunteering. Discounts for children are offered.

Patara Elephant Farm

Patara Elephant Farm has, as Elephant Nature Park, put a lot of focus on rehabilitating abused elephants, but they also offer rides and jungle treks. Apart from the treks, there are two packages that can be booked. The shorter one, which is called Elephant Day Care, lasts for approximately 4 to 5 hours, and as a participant in this program you are allowed to care for your own elephant under the supervision of a professional mahout (trainer). The somewhat longer program, which is called Elephant Owner for a Day, lasts 6 to 8 hours and is about taking care of your own elephant for a whole day, which might include feeding it, administering medicine, practicing various skills, bathing, as well as going on treks. You are also taught how to communicate with elephants, and this theoretical knowledge can later on during the day be applied practically.

The two programs must be booked in advance since it is one elephant per paying customer. Patara Elephant Farm lies much closer to Chiang Mai than Elephant Nature Park.

Directions: The easiest way to get to Patara Elephant Farm is by your own vehicle, or some kind of taxi. The Farm is located on route 1269, approximately 30 kilometers outside Chiang Mai, by the national park Doi Suthep.
Opening hours: All year round depending on booking arrangements.
Fees: Treks start at around 800 baht. Elephant Day Care 3 800 baht. Elephant Owner for a Day 5 800 baht.

Mae Sa Elephant Camp

Mae Sa Elephant Camp is, as the two abovementioned elephant farms are, also involved in the protection of elephants, but the emphasis is nevertheless a bit more on entertainment and tourism. At Mae Sa, visitors are offered rides, jungle treks, the opportunity to swim and bathe with the elephants, as well as shows where you get to paint actual pictures together with the elephants. In addition, shorter courses in becoming a mahout/elephant trainer are offered, similar to the more advanced courses provided by Patara Elephant Farm.

Directions: The easiest way to get to Mae Sa Elephant Camp is by your own vehicle, or some kind of taxi. Leave Chiang Mai to the north via route 107, and drive approximately 20 kilometers. Turn left on route 1096, and then continue for another 10 kilometers.
Opening hours: Daily 08.00 – 16.00.
Admission fees: The elephant show costs 200 baht for adults and 100 baht for children. Elephant treks for two persons cost 800 baht. The cost of the mahout training depends on the content and length of the course.

Flight of the Gibbon: Ziplining

The company Flight of the Gibbon arranges various forms of adventure treks, including caving, mountain climbing, kayaking, and mountain biking in absolutely stunning environments. These alternatives are, in many cases, too physically demanding for the youngest members of a family. However, something that does suit the whole family, as long as you are over one meter tall and weigh less than 130 kilos, is the five-kilometer-long zipline course in the jungle canopies.

The course zigzags through the majestic trees via a system of cables, harnesses, and platforms. There are altogether 33 platforms and suspension bridges, where the longest distance between two of them is a whopping 800 meters, creating the sensation of actually flying. Guides tag along on the tour and there will be many opportunities to see and meet wild monkeys, birds, and other interesting species living in the treetops of northern Thailand.

Directions: Since the course usually must be booked in advance, transfer to and from the guests' hotels are included in the price. Booking arrangements can be done via the website of the company or at a local travel agency.

Opening hours: Pick up and drop off at any Chiang Mai hotel from early morning to late afternoon.
Fees: Ziplining with free transfer from 3 599 baht per person.

Flights over Chiang Mai

If you would like to experience Chiang Mai, along with the thick and luscious jungles, as well as the majestic mountains, from a completely unique and different perspective, then you might be interested in going for a flight over the area.

In Chiang Mai, two flight options are offered, both being secure and certified. The first one is Balloon Adventure Thailand, which is partly governed by Chiang Mai Airport Tower, offering daytrips in hot air balloons. The second alternative is Chiang Mai Sky Adventure, where they arrange flights in micro airplanes with enough space for two persons. There are, however, weight limitations. In addition, the company also offers trips in hot air balloons.

Both companies are open all year round. Nevertheless, the flights are, for obvious reasons, dependent on weather conditions, meaning that some flights might be cancelled during the monsoon season.

Directions: Transfer to and from any hotel in Chiang Mai is usually included in the price. Bookings are done via the websites of the companies or at local travel agencies.
Opening hours: All year round.
Fees: The price starts at around 1 500 – 3 000 baht per person.

Jungle Bungy Jump

Not far from Chiang Mai lies Jungle Bungy Jump, where everyone who is daring enough can jump from a 50-meter-high tower under the supervision of professional and experienced staff. All bungee jumps are filmed, and

DVDs and t-shirts of the jumps can later be purchased. The management at Jungle Bungy Jump also offers night jumps. Jungle Bungy Jump is a franchise business with branches all over Thailand. The company is fully insured and follows safety standards from New Zealand. Although there are no age restrictions, to be able to jump you must weigh at least 35 kilos, but less than 235 kilos, if doing a tandem jump.

On the premises, there is also a mini-zoo, where the younger members of the family can play and cuddle with, among other small animals, guinea pigs. The location of Jungle Bungy Jump is ideal for a combination of activities, as it is situated at Mae Sa, where you can find both wonderful waterfalls and exciting snake shows.

Directions: The easiest way to get to Jungle Bungy Jump is by using the free shuttle bus service of the company, which can be booked online or via local travel agencies. If driving, head towards Mae Rim on route 107, then turn left towards Sa Moeng.
Opening hours: Daily 09.00 – 18.00 (night jumps are available).
Admission fees: Bungee jump with complimentary souvenir for 2000 – 2400 baht.

Mae Sa Snake Farm

At Mae Sa Snake Farm, you are allowed to both touch and hold all sorts of different snakes. In addition, a really exciting and thrilling show is put on three times daily, where the snake handlers let the audience get really, really close to the snakes, including the venomous ones.

Although emphasis is put on entertainment, some research and breeding activities are carried out at Mae Sa Snake Farm, especially regarding endangered species. However, as with all animal shows in Thailand, some of it might not be on par with western expectations.

Directions: The easiest way to get to Mae Sa Snake Farm is by your own vehicle, or some kind of taxi. Drive north on route 107 for approximately

20 kilometers, then turn left on route 1096, and continue for another couple of kilometers.
Opening hours: Daily 09.00 – 17.00.
Admission fees: Adults 200 baht. Children 100 baht.

Mini-Golf

Something most families like to enjoy together is a good game of mini-golf. And in Chiang Mai, you will find two courses of a very high standard.

Inter Mini-Golf

At Golden Elephant Resort, just southeast of central Chiang Mai, lies Inter Mini-Golf, which is an 18-hole course with a very nice finish located in a particularly pleasant and beautiful setting. Around all the holes, there are plenty of planted trees, providing shade for the players, which is most welcomed during hot and sunny days.

Directions: The easiest way to get to Inter Mini-Golf is by your own vehicle, or some kind of taxi. The course lies about 10 kilometers southeast of central Chiang Mai by route 1317. Drive south on route 11, turn left at route 121, then make a right, before route 1317, towards Inter Mini-Golf/Golden Elephant Resort.
Opening hours: Daily 09.00 – 22.00.
Admission fees: Adults 100 baht. Children 60 baht.

Hansa Mini-Golf: Discover the World of Wonders

Hansa Mini-Golf is considered by many to be one of the most beautiful mini-golf courses in Thailand. The course is constructed around world-famous landmarks and buildings, letting you play against the backdrop of, for example, the Statue of Liberty in New York, Stonehenge in England, and the Eiffel Tower in Paris. It is elaborate and innovative, turning the trip into something more than just an ordinary game of mini-golf.

Directions: The easiest way to get to Hansa Mini-Golf is by your own vehicle, or some kind of taxi. Leave Chiang Mai to the north via route 1367, drive approximately 12 kilometers to the intersection at route 3012, then turn right and continue for another couple of kilometers.
Opening hours: Friday to Monday 10.00 – 20.00.
Admission fees: Adults 100 baht. 30 baht for children under the age of 12.

Night Safari

Despite its name, Chiang Mai Night Safari also consists of a part that is open daytime. The daytime tour is called Jaguar Trail Zone, and it is a 1.2-kilometer-long hike around a lake where over 400 animals, such as white tigers, leopards, camels, monkeys, and tapirs, roam free. In addition, there are Segways to rent in case the walk feels a bit too long in the heat.

The night safari, however, is divided into two sections, Savanna Safari Zone, and Predator Prowl Zone. In both these sections, you travel through the area in specially designed pickups that are open on their sides. Both trips are approximately five kilometers long, and take about an hour to complete, respectively. In Savana Safari Zone, you will be able to see, among other animals, giraffes, zebras, rhinos, wildebeests, water buffalos, hyenas, and cheetahs. The animals in Predator Prowl Zone are, on the other hand, exclusively carnivores, for example, tigers, lions, vultures, wolfs, bears, and crocodiles. All dangerous animals are prohibited from coming too close to the pickup.

Apart from the safari trips, there are several other entertaining venues at the spot, such as the Nightly Musical Fountain Show, and Water Screen Laser Light Show, in addition to a cabaret and dinner show. Moreover, a small photo section has been put up where the guests can take pictures of themselves with lion and tiger cubs. Nearby, as an added bonus, you will find the large playground of Fun Plaza.

Directions: The easiest way to get to Chiang Mai Night Safari is by your own vehicle, or some kind of taxi. Leave Chiang Mai to the west via route 3029, drive for approximately 14 kilometers, then turn on to route 3044. There are, however, free shuttle buses departing from outside the Tourist Police at the Night Bazaar.
Opening hours: Jaguar Trail Zone daily 11.00 – 22.00. Savanna Safari Zone/Predator Prowl Zone daily 18.00 – 23.30. Musical Fountain and Laser Light Show daily at 20.00 and 21.00. Cabaret daily at 17.30 and 21.00.
Admission fees Jaguar Trail Zone: Adults 100 baht. Children (100 cm – 140 cm) 50 baht. Free admission for children under 100 cm.
Admission fees Savanna Safari Zone/Predator Prowl Zone: Adults 800 baht. Children (100 cm – 140 cm) 400 baht. Free admission for children under 100 cm.

Night Bazaar

Chiang Mai's biggest outdoor market is Chiang Mai Night Bazaar. During the day, just an ordinary street. At night, however, a kilometer-long shopping bonanza. As with many other large outdoor markets in Thailand, for example, the ones in Hua Hin, it is not only the actual shopping that lures, but also all that comes with it. Chiang Mai Night Bazaar is a place that is absolutely teeming with life and you will find restaurants, street kitchens, mom and pop shops, and local vendors selling all sorts of bric-a-bracs mixed in with the many market stalls.

At Chiang Mai Night Bazaar, you need to haggle, but always tongue in cheek. The general atmosphere is truly pleasant, and most often there will be artists and musicians present making it all a bit livelier. Furthermore, do not forget to explore all the back alleys connecting to the main shopping street, as the real gems are usually found off the beaten track.

Directions: The easiest way to get to Chiang Mai Night Bazaar is on foot as the market lies close to Tha Phae Gate in central Chiang Mai.
Opening hours: Daily 18.00 – 24.00.

Admission fees: There are no admission fees for Chiang Mai Night Bazaar.

Queen Sirikit Botanic Garden

Queen Sirikit Botanic Garden is one of Thailand's biggest botanical gardens, and here you will not only experience the flora of Thailand, but also the flora of more foreign ecosystems. The area is vast and consists of a number of pathways leading through fantastic gardens, waterfalls, and plantations. In addition, there are a couple of huge conservatories with both domestic and foreign plants and flowers, for example, one with cactuses from North and South America, and another one with only carnivorous plants.

The most fun activity for the children, though, might be the raised pathway through the treetops of the jungle-like garden. There is also the possibility to spend the night at Queen Sirikit Botanic Garden, and the hotel comes with both a swimming pool and large playgrounds.

Directions: The easiest way to get to Queen Sirikit Botanic Garden is by your own vehicle, or some kind of taxi. Leave Chiang Mai to the north via route 107 and drive approximately 20 kilometers, then turn left on route 1096, and continue for another 10 kilometers.
Opening hours: Daily 08.30 – 17.00.
Admission fees: Adults 100 baht. Children 50 baht.

Rivers of Chiang Mai

Exploring the rivers surrounding Chiang Mai can be both truly thrilling and extremely relaxing. The two most common options of discovering, and enjoying, the waterways of Chiang Mai are white water rafting and bamboo rafting.

White Water Rafting

The geographical location of Chiang Mai makes it very suitable for white water rafting trips. Most of the excursions are arranged along the Mae Tang river and are offered with various levels of difficulty, requiring various levels of skills and endurance. Some sections of the river suit the whole family, while others are only for the truly adventurous ones. Most trips will be combined with swimming in waterfalls and nice picnics. Moreover, local travel agencies can also arrange white water rafting higher up in the mountains along with jungle treks and camping.

There are many tour companies in the market, but the websites of some of the larger ones, for example, Chiang Mai Adventure, as well as Siam Rivers, offer good examples of what you can do in and around Chiang Mai if interested in adventure tours and white water rafting.

Bamboo Rafting

Contrary to white water rafting, so-called bamboo rafting is a very relaxing and peaceful way of experiencing the stunning nature surrounding Chiang Mai. Along the calmer parts of the river, guests are taken for a gentle tour of the landscape on rafts made out of bamboo with comfortable chairs attached to them.

The rafts are rather small and can only carry a few people at a time. They are maneuvered by guides with the aid of the light currents and a paddle. Plenty of opportunities are provided for swimming, sunbathing, and nice picnics.

Directions: Most of the tours are located somewhere on the Mae Tang river, however, not all of them. Check availability at local travel agencies or via the websites of the abovementioned companies.

Opening hours: Open all year round, but with fewer trips scheduled during the monsoon season.

Fees: White water rafting and bamboo rafting usually start at 800 baht per person. Discounts are offered when combining activities.

Segways in Chiang Mai

The company running the zipline course Flight of the Gibbon also arranges tours through downtown Chiang Mai on Segways. The trip is two hours long, and every group is accompanied by guides on their own Segways. No prior experience is needed, since guests are allowed to practice handling the vehicle before setting out. Even relatively small children are able to control a Segway after some training. The only requirements are that the participants must not weigh less than 40 kilos or more than 113 kilos.

Exploring Chiang Mai by Segway is both comfortable and practical, making it easier to reach and discover places that otherwise might be hard to find. The Segway tour can be combined with a trip to the zipline course at a greatly reduced price. Snacks and drinks are included in the fee for the trip. If showing up with a big entourage, it should be noted that there is a maximum of six participants per group and instructor.

Directions: The easiest way to get to Chiang Mai Segway Tours is on foot as they are located in central Chiang Mai, opposite the Tha Pae Gate. During high-season, it is recommended to book in advance.
Opening hours: Daily from morning to late night.
Fees: 1 999 baht per Segway and participant.

Swimming and Water Play

Even though Chiang Mai is located in the mountains of northern Thailand, there are plenty of chances to go swimming at some really spectacular spots.

The Waterfalls of Chiang Mai

Around Chiang Mai, you will be able to find several big and small waterfalls with both deep and shallow pools of fresh water. The closest one is right outside Chiang Mai at the mountain of Doi Suthep, where you also have the opportunity to visit one of Thailand's most famous temples. Other waterfalls, which are a bit more spectacular, are located within a comfortable driving distance of the city. Many of them are divided into several levels, where you might have to do a bit of climbing to access the best ones, particularly if you enjoy cliff diving.

The easiest way of finding waterfalls suitable for young children is to visit any of the small travel agencies that have set up shop around town. On the other hand, most waterfalls are quite safe at their lower levels, and there should not be any problems with exploring them by yourself. At some waterfalls, visitors must pay an entrance fee since they are located within national parks. The fee is usually 200 – 400 baht. Another thing to keep in mind is that the water level shifts a lot during the monsoon season.

Trips to the waterfalls can easily be combined with other fun activities. Mae Sa Waterfall, for example, is not far from Mae Snake Farm and Jungle Bungy Jump.

San Kamphaeng Hot Springs

There are several hot springs scattered around the mountains with spouting fountains and impressive geysers. The most visited is called San Kamphaeng Hot Springs and lies approximately 30 kilometers outside Chiang Mai. At San Kamphaeng Hot Springs you can take baths in private barrels, huge tubs, or small pools where the hot water has been mixed with cool fresh water. The water is believed to be very good for your skin as it has an unusually high concentration of minerals.

Another fun activity is to buy some eggs at the premises and then boil them yourself for lunch in one of the geysers. In addition, there are bungalows to rent if you are interested in staying the night. If looking for a more luxurious hotel, you have the option of Roon Arun Hot Springs Resort, which is just around the corner from San Kamphaeng Hot Springs.

Directions: The easiest way to get to San Kamphaeng Hot Springs, located east of Chiang Mai along route 1317, is by your own vehicle or some kind of taxi. You could also take the local bus from Chang Phuak bus terminal in Chiang Mai to nearby San Kamphaeng.
Opening hours: Daily 08.00 – 21.00.
Admission fees: Adults 30 baht and children 15 baht. Bathe in a big barrel: 15 baht for 30 minutes. Bathe in a big tub: 30 baht for 30 minutes. Bathe in a mini pool (a maximum of 10 people at a time): 200 baht for 60 minutes.

Tiger Kingdom

North of Chiang Mai lies Tiger Kingdom, which is a branch of Tiger Kingdom in the province of Ubon Rachathani in the northeast of the country, where it is known as Ubon Zoo. At Tiger Kingdom in Chiang Mai, a large number of tigers have been born and bred on the premises. Each tiger has been reared by a personal trainer, which raises certain moral questions since that prevents the tigers from ever being released into the wild. The tigers at Tiger Kingdom have been domesticated to such a high degree that it is possible for the visitors to enter their compounds to touch and take photos.

The area is big and as a visitor you only book the pens and tigers that you wish to visit, usually for ten minutes at a time. Although calm and docile, the larger tigers can be truly intimidating, while the tiger cubs are just as playful as ordinary cats. The trainers are always present, which is comforting since there are no fences separating the visitors from the tigers once you have entered their pens.

Directions: The easiest way to get to Tiger Kingdom is by your own vehicle, or some kind of taxi. Leave Chiang Mai to the north via route 107, drive approximately 20 kilometers, and then turn left on route 1096.
Opening hours: Daily 09.00 – 18.00.
Fees: The fee is based on the number of tigers you want to visit, as well as on the sizes of them. A visit will probably cost 500 – 1 000 baht per person. Discounts are available.

At the present, following requirements are in effect:

1) *To meet the big tigers, the visitor must be at least 18 years old and 160 centimeters tall*
2) *To meet the middle-sized tigers, the visitor must be at least 15 years old and 160 centimeters tall*
3) *To meet the small tigers, the visitor must be at least 140 centimeters tall*
4) *To meet the white tigers, the visitor must be at least 150 centimeters tall*
5) *There are no requirements for meeting the tiger cubs*

Tubing on Mae Ping River

White water rafting and bamboo rafting are two very popular ways of exploring the many rivers and streams surrounding Chiang Mai. There is, however, a third alternative, namely Tubing. The company Chiang Mai Tubing & Beach Club arranges specially constructed swimming rings with built-in neck support and beverage compartments, allowing the guests to leisurely drift down the river while taking in the truly amazing nature lining the banks of the waterways.

A set of straps comes with the ring so that families and friends can tie their rings together, forming a huge raft. In addition, floating cool bags are included in the rent, making it possible to bring chilled drinks with you on the trip. Tubing is extremely comfortable and fun since you have the opportunity to sunbath and swim as much as you want while drifting along the river. At the Beach Club, several activities besides tubing are offered, for example, badminton, volleyball, and horseshoe pitching.

Directions: The easiest way to get to Chiang Mai Tubing & Beach Club is by using the free shuttle bus service of the company.
Opening hours: Daily from early morning to late night.
Fees: 599 baht per person. Group discounts are offered.

Hua Hin and Cha-Am

Approximately 230 kilometers south of Bangkok lie the two cities of Hua Hin and Cha-Am, connected to each other by an infinitely long beach. And it is the child-friendly beach, among a host of other intriguing qualities, that year after year attracts the tourists, foreign as well as local.

In addition, Hua Hin and Cha-Am are easy to get around in, even for families traveling with very young children. Moreover, both communities, but in particular Hua Hin, are much calmer than many other coastal towns in Thailand. The Royal Family has a large summer residence near the city, which has led to the whole area being a bit cleaner and more well-kept, not to mention safer and cheaper, than its counterparts Phuket and Koh Samui.

Hua Hin and Cha-Am are two towns with a tendency to lure tourists back for a second visit, as well as for a third, fourth, and fifth. Here you can find a combination of the best Thailand has got to offer: endlessly long and child-friendly beaches, fun excursion and activities for both young and old, strange temples and odd outings, interesting markets of all sizes and, not least, a genuinely open-minded and welcoming local population.

Hua Hin and Cha-Am belong to those rare places where a positive exchange between tourism and tradition has evolved, and keeps flourishing.

Beach Activities

The beach between Hua Hin and Cha-Am is really long, and it does not ever come to an absolute end. Instead, it is divided into smaller sections by either natural obstacles, such as hills, or residential neighborhoods. Just south of Hua Hin, for example, the beach ends at the mountainous rock formation of Khao Takiab, but continues, nevertheless, on the other side for another couple of kilometers, until the next natural barrier.

By using your own vehicle, you can easily find a private oasis by the sea. If, on the other hand, you are looking for fun and exciting activities, then there are numerous things to do on a day at the beach. During the high season, you can expect to find banana boats, kayaks, jet skis, and SUPs (Stand Up Paddle Boards), as well as companies offering kitesurfing and kiteboarding. Considering that it hardly ever stops blowing at the beaches of Hua Hin and Cha-Am, both kitesurfing and kiteboarding have become trademark sports of these two coastal towns.

None of the abovementioned activities need to be booked in advance, and the price usually starts at around a couple of hundred baht per person and activity. Furthermore, all beach activities, including swimming and snorkeling, are most enjoyable between October and May. During the monsoon season, most beach activities shut down.

Black Mountain Mini-Golf & Wakeboard Park

Around Hua Hin, there are several big golf courses of a high international standard. Nonetheless, a game of golf is not always something that everyone in the family enjoys. At Black Mountain, though, there is not only an award-winning golf course, but also a mini-golf course, volleyball courts, and boule lanes, in addition to Black Mountain Water Park (see section Water Parks). One of the most exciting attractions at Black Mountain is, on the other hand, the Wakeboard Park.

When wakeboarding, you are not following a speed boat on a pair of water-skies. Instead, you use a board similar to a snowboard. Moreover, the boat is replaced by a cable system that you hook yourself up to so that it can drag you along an artificial lake. The wakeboard park at Black Mountain suits both absolute beginners and more advanced riders. Although wakeboarding in general does not require any previous experience, it might be a bit too physically demanding for the younger members of the family.

Additionally, at Black Mountain you will also find spas, tennis courts, gyms, and luxurious hotel rooms. This is a first-class resort with reasonable prices, especially if you are only going to use their facilities.

Directions: The easiest way to get to Black Mountain is by your own vehicle, or some kind of taxi. Black Mountain lies approximately 15 kilometers west of Hua Hin. Leave town by soi 70, turn left on route 3218, then turn right on route 1049, and continue for another 10 kilometers.
Opening hours: Daily 10.00 – 18.00 (the opening hours vary depending on activity. The golf course, for example, opens much earlier).
Fees: Wakeboarding 2 hours for 600 baht, 4 hours for 900 baht, the whole day for 1 200 baht.

Black Sheep Farm

About 20 kilometers west of Hua Hin lies the little farm Black Sheep Farm. Visitors to this farm can expect to meet and feed sheep, goats, ducks, deer, fish, and rabbits. The area is well-kept and the animals are healthy and allowed to move around in pens and enclosures of descent sizes. Since some of the animals run free, for example, very playful young goats and extremely large ducks, Black Sheep Farm is well suited for families who want to get really close to animals.

Considering that the farm is rather small, a visit does not last for more than an hour or so. In the vicinity, however, lies the well-known and nationally famous temple Wat Huay Mongkol, boasting its immensely large statue of the monk Luang Phor Toad. The temple grounds are located in a park with beautiful waterways and pathways. A trip to Black Sheep Farm, in combination with a visit to the temple Wat Huay Mongkol, makes for a nice whole-day excursion.

Directions: The easiest way to get to Black Sheep farm is by your own vehicle, or some kind of taxi. Leave Hua Hin via soi 70, turn right on route 3218, and continue towards Wat Huay Mongkol. Just before reaching the temple, turn left at the intersection, and then make a right turn after approximately 500 meters.
Opening hours: Daily 09.00 – 17.00.
Admission fees: Adults 50 baht. Children (under the age of 10) 30 baht. No admission fees for visiting the temple.

Boating and Fishing Trips

Both Hua Hin and Cha-Am are coastal towns, meaning that there are plenty of opportunities for going on boat trips, or to do some fishing. When it comes to fishing, there are two options: either fish in the sea by boat, or fish at any of the artificial lakes in the area.

If you choose to go deep sea fishing, bear in mind that this should only be done during the high season. That is to say, between October and April – you really do not want to be caught in a boat when the yearly monsoon passes by. If you are interested in combining fishing with swimming and snorkeling, then you are recommended to take a trip to the small but unexploited island of Singtho, which is visible from the beach in Hua Hin. There are numerous local travel agencies in both Hua Hin and Cha-Am that arrange outings of this sort.

However, if opting for fishing for freshwater fish, you can do this all year round. The best artificial fishing lake in the area is Hua Hin Fishing Lodge. Here they have created two lakes with over forty different species, ranging from really small ones to some of the absolutely biggest, for example, the giant Arapaima. You do not need to bring your own gear, since everything can be rented at the lake. On the premises, there is a playground for the kids. Guests also have the option of spending the night in modern bungalows right next to the lake.

Directions: The easiest way to get to Hua Hin Fishing Lodge is by your own vehicle, or some kind of taxi. Leave Hua Hin via soi 70, turn right on route 3218, drive for a couple of kilometers, turn again at route 1049, and then continue for another couple of kilometers.

Opening hours: Daily from morning to late night.

Fees: Day fishing at the lake with fish weighing a maximum of 25 kilos costs 600 baht for adults and 300 baht for children. Day fishing at the lake with the largest species costs 1 500 baht per person. Night fishing is charged extra. However, if booking a bungalow, discounts are usually offered.

Camel Republic Cha-Am

Something that has become a kind of trademark of Hua Hin and Cha-Am is the large number of theme parks. Camel Republic is one of them, and as with many other theme parks in Thailand, it is a combination of a zoo and a funfair.

In the park, as the name implies, you will find various animals from the Middle East, for example, alpacas and camels, which you can feed and go for a ride with. Other interesting animals include the giraffes and the flamingos, as well as a large number of various species of parrots, which are kept in huge cages. For a small fee, you are allowed to step inside the enclosures to feed these really playful birds.

The funfair is a bit small but, on the other hand, quite modern with a new take on several classic rides. Furthermore, there are gaming arcades, bouncy castles, 4D movies, ziplines, and more. At Camel Republic, everyone in the family can find something fun to do. In addition, the park is located within a stone's throw of several other big and fun tourist destinations in Cha-Am.

Directions: The easiest way to get to Camel Republic is by your own vehicle, or some kind of taxi. Alternatively, get on one of the red an orange local buses that run between Hua Hin and Cha-Am. Camel Republic is located on route 4, just north of Cha-Am, opposite Santorini Park, and next to Swiss Sheep Farm.
Opening hours: Monday to Friday 10.00 – 18.00. Saturday and Sunday 09.00 – 18.30.
Admission fees: Adults 150 baht. Free admission for children under 100 cm. Most of the rides/activities cost 100 – 200 baht per person.

Cha-Am ATV Park

Between Hua Hin and Cha-Am lies Cha-Am ATV Park. Here you can drive all sorts of different ATVs. The tracks are, in addition, suited for both complete beginners and skilled professionals. If you are looking for a more challenging course, then there is the option of driving outside the actual premises, navigating tracks with natural obstacles and hurdles, such as creeks and forest hills.

Cha-Am ATV Park is also a popular destination for people who enjoy paintball. The paintball range is large enough to allow really big parties playing at the same time. Furthermore, at the premises there are horses, which you can go for a ride with in the surrounding area. Another big pull of the park is the archery range. Cha-Am ATV Park is, despite its name, so much more than just ATVs. Here you can spend the whole day, regardless of your age.

Directions: The easiest way to get to Cha-Am ATV Park is by your own vehicle, or some kind of taxi. Alternatively, get on one of the red and orange local buses that run between Cha-Am and Hua Hin. The park is located approximately 20 kilometers north of Hua Hin along route 4.
Opening hours: Daily 09.00 – 18.00 (closed Wednesdays according to the website of the company).

Fees: Paintball starts at 600 baht per person. Archery starts at 400 baht per person. ATVs start at 1 000 baht per vehicle.

Go Kart Hua Hin

On the tracks of Go Kart Hua Hin, both adults and children can find something that suit them and their skills. The tracks, as well as the vehicles and their engine sizes, are very varied, making it possible to adjust the level of difficulty to each person's age and competence. In addition, there are special slots allotted to the youngest drivers, although not younger than 7 years old. These timeslots are not fixed, and it might be a good idea to check the website of the company before showing up with really young participants. It is also recommended to book in advance if you plan to drive in larger groups.

Moreover, there are two-seated go-karts available so that absolutely everyone can go for a ride, regardless of driving skills or age. At Go Kart Hua Hin, competitions are arranged regularly, and they are open for the public. The most spectacular one is the Full Moon Race, and, as the name implies, it takes place only once a month.

Directions: The easiest way to get to Go Kart Hua Hin is by your own vehicle, or some kind of taxi. Alternatively, the local red and orange buses, as well as the green pickup taxis, stop close to the tracks. Go Kart Hua Hin is located opposite soi 2.
Opening hours: Daily 10.30 – 19.00 (night visits can be booked separately).
Fees: The cost varies according to vehicle, engine size, and length of time. It starts, however, at around 400 baht per person.

Hua Hin Horse Club

If you like horses, there are several options to choose from at Hua Hin and Cha-Am. On the beach, for example, you can go for a horse ride for 20 to

60 minutes at a cost of 300 to 800 baht. If you, on the other hand, are interested in participating in longer excursions with horses from local stables, then Hua Hin Horse Club might be something for you.

At this stable, both half day and full day horse rides and treks are offered, in addition to shorter trips for absolute beginners. The excursions, rides, and treks can be arranged in groups or privately. Moreover, children under the age of sixteen are invited to help out with grooming the horses. One of the most popular treks is the trip to Khao Tao Lake, which includes a quick stop at the sea for some bathing with the horses. The excursion lasts for approximately four hours. All treks and trips can be adjusted to suit both absolute beginners and professional riders.

Directions: The easiest way to get to Hua Hin Horse Club is by your own vehicle, or some kind of taxi. The stable is located a couple of kilometers south of central Hua Hin, between soi 114 and 116.
Opening hours: From early morning to late night according to bookings and arrangements.
Fees: The cost ranges from 800 – 2 000 baht depending on length of time and if you are going to go on a trek or plan to take riding lessons.

Hua Hin Safari & Adventure Park

Just south of Hua Hin lies Hua Hin Safari & Adventure Park, where the management has put together a host of activities in one and the same place. The list of things to do is long. The most popular activities are, however, the safari trip, and elephant trekking in the surrounding hills and forests. If you do not want to ride an elephant, there is the option of horses, and most of the excursions, regardless of animal, are between 30 minutes and 2 hours long. No prior experience needed.

A more comfortable alternative of exploring the landscape is, though, by horse and carriage, which includes a stop at the park's own pineapple plantation. In addition to various treks and trips, there are also ATVs to hire, which you can take for a spin either in the park or along forest pathways in the surrounding area. At the park, you will also find a large paintball range.

Hua Hin Safari & Adventure Park is quite big, and if none of the above-mentioned activities suit you, then there is always the option of going to see the snake, elephant, and crocodiles shows that are put on daily.

Directions: The easiest way to get to Hua Hin Safari & Adventure Park is by using the free shuttle bus service of the company, which can be ordered to most hotels in Hua Hin. If driving, follow route 4 south of Hua Hin, and then turn right towards the hills after passing Banyan Golf Park.
Opening hours: Daily 08.00 – 17.00.
Fees: The cost vary depending on activity. However, no trip or trek should cost more than approximately 1 000 baht per person. Group discounts are offered.

Huai Sai Wildlife Breeding Center

At first glance, Huai Sai Wildlife Breeding Center seems to be an ordinary small zoo, however, this is not the case. Huai Sai Wildlife Breeding Center is more like a large farm, under so-called Royal Protection, where the management breed endangered animals, such as exotic birds, various species of monkeys, deer, and porcupines, whilst preparing them for being released into the wild.

The animals are well looked after and can roam freely in relatively large enclosures. The monkeys, for example, have their own little islands at the far end of the park – some, though, are in cages due to vaccinations and other related issues. Huai Sai Wildlife Breeding Center suits everyone in the family who is interested in animals, and since it is not a zoo in the usual sense of the word, it is very quiet and calm. Bear in mind, though, that there are no restaurants in the area, only a small shop where you can buy beverages, fruit, grass, and vegetables for the animals.

Directions: The easiest way to get to Huai Sai Wildlife Breeding Center is by your own vehicle, or some kind of taxi. Leave Hua Hin north via route 4, drive towards Cha-Am for about 10 kilometers, then turn left on route 1010. Continue for another 4 kilometers. Huai Sai Wildlife Breeding Center is on the left-hand side.
Opening hours: Daily 08.00 – 16.30.
Admission fees: Free admission for everyone.

Hutsadin Elephant Foundation

Just west of Hun Hin, there is a non-profit organization for mistreated, abused, and abandoned elephants. The staff consists of experienced elephant trainers – so-called mahouts – university educated veterinarians, and volunteers. Since the organization cannot survive solely on the donations received, the management has started to arrange some activities for tourists in a bid to secure enough funds to provide for the elephants.

The main attraction is elephant trekking around the nearby jungle hills. There is the option or riding bareback, as well as swimming with the elephants. In addition, guests are invited to enjoy a nice show with some of the younger elephants on the premises. Another exciting activity, which is only offered to adults, is practicing as a mahout. If signing up for a short course, you will have the opportunity of participating in all the daily routines regarding taking care of an elephant, which might include administering medicine and arranging the meals. During high season, practicing as a mahout usually needs to be booked in advance.

Directions: The easiest way to get to Hutsadin Elephant Foundation is by your own vehicle, or some kind of taxi. Leave Hua Hin via soi 70, turn right on route 3218, and then continue for another couple of kilometers.
Opening hours: Daily 09.00 – 18.00.
Fees for adults: 1-hour trek 800 baht. ½ hour trek 600 baht. Mahout training for 3 hours 1 000 baht. Elephant show 300 baht. Ride bareback for 20 minutes, including swimming with the elephants, 1 000 baht.

Fees for children: 1-hour trek 600 baht. ½ hour trek 400 baht. Elephant show 150 baht. Ride bareback, including swimming with the elephants, 1000 baht.

Khao Takiab and the Monkey Temple

The mountainous hill of Khao Takiab, which is clearly visible from central Hua Hin, lies in the far south end of the beach. And if you choose to walk all the way, bear in mind that you will probably need both a sunhat and plenty of sunscreen.

On top of the hill, there is a unique temple which locally is called the Monkey Temple. As the name implies, at times the temple grounds are absolutely littered with big and small macaques. Now and again, the monkeys get really bold and pushy, and you should hold on tightly to any handbags or, more importantly, food containers.

The temple, and its surroundings, is fascinating, and the first thing you see when visiting the area is a twenty-meter-high golden Buddha statue, marking the entrance to the temple stairway that has been carved out of the rock. As an added bonus, there are beautiful beaches on both sides of the hill, where you can rent jet skis and kiteboards, go for a ride on banana boats, or just relax and sunbathe.

Directions: The easiest way to get to Khao Takiab is by the green pickup taxis from central Hua Hin. Khao Takiab is the last stop on their route.
Opening hours: From early morning to after sunset.
Admission fees: There are no admission fees.

Magic Balloon Park

Magic Balloon Park is located just outside Cha-Am. At Magic Balloon Park you can without a doubt take some of the best pictures, and enjoy some of the best views, in vertical balloon trips. That is, in balloons that are firmly anchored to the ground. In order to make the trips as safe as possible, the company uses enormous helium balloons instead of hot air balloons, and the biggest baskets can take up to twenty people. The balloons rise to approximately 100 meters, and stay in place by robust wires. In addition, every guest must wear a safety harness to prevent anyone from falling out of the basket. The company is insured, and all trips are cancelled with a refund in case of bad weather.

The most popular flights take place either in the morning around sunrise, or in the afternoon around sunset. During the high season, booking in advance is recommended if you want to fly in the most sought-after timeslots. On the premises, there is also a large playground for the younger kids in the family.

Directions: The easiest way to get to Magic Balloon Park is by your own vehicle, or some kind of taxi. Alternatively, get on the red and orange local bus that runs between Hua Hin and Cha-Am. Magic Balloon Park is located by 1000 Suk Food and Farm, a couple of kilometers north of Cha-Am.
Opening hours: Daily 08.00 – 12.00, and 16.00 – 20.00.
Fees: Adults 550 baht. Children (ages 6 – 12) 300 baht. Free for children under the age of 6.

Markets and Shopping Malls in Hua Hin

In Hua Hin, there are four big night markets, as well as two modern shopping malls, one of which is brand-new.

Hua Hin Night Market & Chatsila Night Market

Located in central Hua Hin, mainly along soi 72, is Hua Hin Night Market. If you are looking for cheap shopping, cheap massages, cheap street food, and cheap authentic sweets and delicacies, this is the place for you. The road is lined with food stalls and market stalls, selling everything imaginable. Hua

Hin Night Market opens at 18.00 every day, and closes around midnight. It is lively and crowded, but also really fun and enjoyable. Having dinner at any of the restaurants behind the throng of market stalls, overlooking the busy street life, is truly entertaining.

In addition, Chatsila Night Market lies adjacent to Hua Hin Night Market. However, the two markets differ a bit from each other. At Chatsila, the focus is not on shopping and food, but rather on shopping and art.

Cicada Market

Located between the hill of Khao Takiab and central Hua Hin is Cicada Market. Contrary to the nightly hustle and bustle of Hua Hin Night Market, Cicada Market is only open from Friday afternoon to late Sunday night. On the other hand, Cicada Market offers so much more than just great shopping venues. At Cicada, you can expect to experience, and enjoy, an exciting and interesting mix of theatrical performances, street artists, traditional shows and cabarets, as well as free concerts. Many of the vendors at Cicada Market are, in fact, artists from local universities and art schools, contributing to the very cultural atmosphere of Cicada.

The market is located in a nice park which, at night, comes to life through sparkling lights and soothing fountains. At Cicada Market, you will find a truly wide range of foods for sale. A large restaurant area has been constructed in the middle of the park, where a multitude of kitchens prepare both western and Asian dishes. At the entrance, you buy food coupons, and then pick up whatever you fancy from any of the numerous mini-restaurants.

Grand Market Hua Hin

Between Cicada Market and Hua Hin Night Market lies Grand Market Hua Hin, right next to the private hospital San Paolo at Petchkasem Road. Grand Market Hua Hin is open daily. The market is a bit more traditional compared to Cicada Market and Hua Hin Night Market; nonetheless, it is just as lively and fun to visit.

At Grand Market Hua Hin, you will find plenty of market stalls selling everything under the sun, and various restaurants of all sizes, as well as massage parlors and bars. It is to this market the Thais usually go at night, which has positively affected the pricing of goods and services. It is somewhat cheaper than competing markets in the area. In addition, the food offered is a bit more Thai than western. At Grand Market Hua Hin, there are a couple of bars that often arrange small-scale concerts and live performances by local rock and pop artists.

Plaern Wan Shopping Village

In north Hua Hin, between soi 38 and soi 40, lies Plaern Wan Shopping Village, which is a very different, but extremely nice, market place. The market is relatively new, but built according to the architectural style of Hua Hin in the 1950s. The transformation of the area, not to mention all the stalls and small shops, is so charming that the "shopping" part of a visit takes a backseat.

Plaern Wan Shopping Village is not, as most other markets are, situated on a plain field or in an open parking lot of some sort, but instead lodged in a whole residential block that has, as mentioned above, been erected in the shape of a traditional village. Plaern Wan Shopping Village is open during the day; however, it is not until night-time that the market comes into its own. In the shopping village, there is also a small outdoor cinema, where visitors can watch movies for free, next to a traditional funfair with games and tombola.

Hua Hin Market Village

A relatively new addition to the shopping scene in Hua Hin is Hua Hin Market Village, which is located about one kilometer south of central Hua

Hin on the main road Petchkasem Road. It is a modern shopping mall with everything that you would expect to find in a similar western counterpart; not least western fast food, in case you have grown tired of the local cuisine. The shops, on the other hand, consist of a mixture of small stands selling mainly cheap Thai brands and large international chains with a wide range of clothes, foods, electronics, and furniture. At Hua Hin Market Village you will also find, among other things, banks, pharmacies, and real estate agents. On the top floor, there is a large arcade with movie theaters, a bowling alley, pool tables, and a big playland for children under the age of 12. The whole shopping mall is air-conditioned; a fact that attracts many visitors on especially hot days.

Blu'Port – Hua Hin Resort Mall

Blu'Port is a brand-new theme based shopping mall where the design reflects beach life and the sea. Both the exterior and the interior are truly impressive, and to let it really dazzle you, why not make sure that your first visit to Blu'Port is after sunset. The façade and surrounding areas are brightly lit up, and the fashionable and luxurious feel to it can rival any upscale shopping mall in Bangkok. Here you will find everything from cool streetwear to top end brand names, in addition to a high number of great food outlets and shopping venues. Furthermore, a lot of money and effort have gone into making Blu'Port fun for kids and teenagers. First and foremost, the cinema and the gaming arcade are state-of-the-art installations. Secondly, Blu'Port can boast of having *"the first interactive underwater world theme park in Thailand"*. This interactive theme park comes, however, with more traditional playgrounds as well, consisting of huge ball pits and large slides, among other fun and thrilling things to do.

The location of Blu'Port Mall is just south of central Hua Hin along the main road, a stone's throw from the competing shopping mall of Hua Hin Market Village.

National Parks

There are two national parks in the vicinity of Hua Hin, both of which are absolutely stunning. If you like to swim in waterfalls, then a visit to the national park of Pala-U is a must. If you, on the other hand, are more into caving and camping, then you should spend some time in Khao Sam Roi Yot National Park.

The Waterfalls of Pala-U

One of Thailand's highest waterfalls is located west of Hua Hin, at the border to Burma. The waterfall is actually a series of waterfalls, divided into sixteen levels. And if you only have the stamina required, you can climb to the very top and be rewarded with a truly magnificent view of the jungles of Burma and Thailand.

The first couple of levels will suffice, though, for families with young children, providing plenty of opportunities to go cliff diving in deep pools, and swimming in shallow ponds with wonderfully cool freshwater. There are plenty of fish in the streams, creaks, and pools of the waterfalls; however, since Pala-U is a national park, all fishing is strictly prohibited. Nonetheless, after long days in the sun by the beaches along the coastline, this a very relaxing and refreshing alternative to the salty sea.

Directions: The easiest way to get to Pala-U is by your own vehicle, or some kind of taxi. Leave Hua Hin via soi 70, turn right on route 3218, and then continue on route 3219 for about 60 kilometers until you reach Pala-U. Alternatively, catch the local bus between Hua Hin and Pala-U, which departs from soi 70.
Opening hours: Daily 08.00 – 17.00.
Admission fees: 50 – 400 baht per person depending on how many levels you would like to access.

Asia Revealed Publishing Company

Khao Sam Roi Yot

At an equally long distance from Hua Hin, though southwards, lies the national park Khao Sam Roi Yot. In this park, you will not find any large waterfalls to swim in; however, there are plenty of untouched and pristine beaches to enjoy.

The park is located in and around a couple of mountainous jungle hills with several wonderful hiking trails to viewpoints over both the park and the sea. Lodged between these hills, there are vast mangroves where you can find many exotic and unusual animal species. Boat services are available at the location, allowing visitors to explore the wetlands for just a few hundred baht. In the hills, which rise from the edge of the sea, there are numerous interesting cave systems. Some with large cavities and hollow hallways, others with long and narrow paths. Furthermore, between the hills and the mangroves lies one of Thailand's biggest freshwater marshes, through which a one-kilometer-long wooden bridge has been erected.

If you would like to spend the night here, there are modern bungalows for rent. A far more exciting alternative, though, is camping at either of the two camping sites.

Directions: The easiest way to get to Khao Sam Roi Yot National Park is by your own vehicle, or some kind of taxi. The northern part of the park is only 27 kilometers south of Hua Hin. Nevertheless, you need to drive another 25 kilometers to get to the main park office. Take route 4 south of Hua Hin towards Pranburi, turn left on route 3168, and continue for another 5 kilometers to route 1020. Once on route 1020, you need to cover an additional 32 kilometers to get to the main office. All the caves and the best beaches are, however, passed long before that.
Opening hours: From early morning to late night.
Admission fees: Visiting Khao Sam Roi Yot is free of charge. There might, however, be a small fee at the cave systems. Staying the night will cost 200 – 2 000 baht depending on the accommodation of your choice.

Palapon Martial Arts & Holistic Fitness Camp

In the south of Hua Hin, just before you reach the hills of Khao Takiab, you will find Palapon Martial Arts & Holistic Fitness Camp, where you can train Thai Boxing, Kung Fu, Yoga, and Tai Chi. The focus of the training is not entirely on the specific branch of martial arts, but rather on creating a mind-set where both body and spirit are taken into consideration.

The training sessions often take place in inspiring locations among the hillside temples or, for example, on the beach at sunset and sunrise. The training offered is not only geared towards adults, but children can also enjoy the highly beneficial practice of martial arts. Moreover, as a family you have the option of tailoring the workout sessions together with a private instructor, so that everyone can participate on their own terms.

Directions: The easiest way to get to Palapon Martial Arts & Holistic Fitness Camp is by the green pickup taxis. The fitness camp is located in the south of central Hua Hin, opposite the weekend market Cicada.
Opening hours: Daily 06.00 – 19.00.
Fees: The cost starts at a few hundred baht per hour. Group discounts are offered. The cost is reduced the more hours you book.

Paramotor Flying Hua Hin

One of the most exciting things you can do when visiting Hua Hin is Paramotor Flying. A paramotor is a small airplane with three wheels, a rotor blade at the back, as well as a kind of parachute attached to the top. The plane takes off by the aid of the propeller, and then gently sails through the air at the chosen altitude.

Paramotor Flying is considered to be one of the safest ways of flying, since you are flying at a low speed, and not too high up in the air. The company's slogan, *"Flying Low and Slow"*, sums up the experience nicely. Only qualified staff work at Paramotor Flying Hua Hin, certified by both

European and American organizations. The actual flying is carried out with two people sitting in the aircraft, the paying customer and the flight instructor, who is maneuvering the plane. No prior experience is needed, and there is no age limit. The activity is open to everyone who is not scared of heights.

Directions: The office, Sky Club Asia, is located near central Hua Hin. Drive south towards Khao Takiab, then turn right at soi 102 to cross the railway tracks. The actual flying takes place at a small airstrip about 30 kilometers south of Hua Hin, near the national park Khao Sam Roi Yot.
Opening hours: Daily from morning to night.
Fees: Standard trip with accompanying instructor costs 3 900 baht per person.

Santorini Park Cha-Am

Right outside Cha-Am, among several other large tourist attractions, lies the somewhat different theme park of Santorini. The park itself has been built according to the architectural style found on a typical Greek island, with a focus on low whitewashed cottages. Santorini Park is the theme park in Hua Hin and Cha-Am that best has managed to recreate the feeling and atmosphere of a foreign place.

The impressive park is divided into three areas: one for shopping, another one for the funfair and the gaming arcades, and a final section dedicated to swimming and sunbathing. In the first area, the main Greek village, there is a wide range of brand stores mixed with local shops carrying cheaper goods, in addition to both Thai and western restaurants, cafés, and ice-cream parlors. The second area is a modern and large amusement park with, among other things, fast rides, 4D and 7D movies, an indoor play area with real snow, and Zorb balls. In the third area, you will find one of the most innovative water parks in Thailand (see section Water Parks).

Directions: The easiest way to get to Santorini Park is by your own vehicle, or some kind of taxi. Alternatively, the red and orange local bus that runs between Hua Hin and Cha-Am stops right outside the entrance of Santorini Park.

Opening hours: Monday to Friday 10.00 – 19.00. Saturday and Sunday 09.00 – 19.00.

Admission fees: Children and adults 150 baht per person. Rides 120 – 240 baht per person.

Sam Phan Nam Floating Market

In Thailand, and especially around Bangkok, floating markets are a common sight, and some of them have become big enough to qualify as real tourist attractions, such as Damnoen Saduak Floating Market and Amphawa Floating Market. In Hua Hin, though, this concept has been expanded and resulted in a Floating Village instead of just a market.

The market place is really big and beautifully decorated, with more than 193 shops lining the banks of the artificial lake in the middle of the floating village, in addition to 40 mini-shops on small boats. There are plenty of nice little restaurants, as well as bakeries and cafes, where you can relax while bobbing in and out of the market stalls. As an added bonus, during high season you can expect to be treated to shows and traditional performances by local artists.

Directions: The easiest way to get to Sam Phan Nam Floating Market is by your own vehicle, or some kind of taxi. Drive southwest from Hua Hin on soi 112. After about 5 kilometers, there will be signs to Sam Phan Nam Floating Market to your left.

Opening hours: Daily 10.00 – 23.00.

Admission fees: Generally, no fees.

Swiss Sheep Farm Cha-Am

Swiss Sheep Farm is located close to Cha-Am, and here you are allowed to get really close to the animals. Swiss Sheep Farm is, however, a theme park, and the concept is that of a so-called typical West European farm, although with a slightly weird end result. At Swiss Sheep Farm, there are not only sheep, but also plenty of exotic species that you would not expect to see in Switzerland.

Besides feeding and playing with the animals on the farm, there are several other fun activities to engage in. For example, going on a tour of the area in a horse and carriage, or picking up a bow and arrow for some archery. The park is well suited for picnics, and you can either bring your own food or buy it from one of the many small restaurants in the area. In addition, Swiss Sheep Farm has, for some odd reason, become very popular among couples in love and newlyweds. And more often than not, you will see whole wedding entourages, along with wedding photographers, running around in the park.

Directions: The easiest way to get to Swiss Sheep Farm is by your own vehicle, or some kind of taxi. Alternatively, take the red and orange local bus that runs between Cha-Am and Hua Hin. The farm is located on route 4, opposite Santorini Park, just north of Cha-Am.
Opening hours: Monday to Friday 10.00 – 19.00. Saturday and Sunday 09.00 – 19.00.
Admission fees: Adults 50 baht. Children 30 baht.

The Venezia

One of the biggest theme parks in Hua Hin and Cha-Am is The Venezia. The area has been built according to the architectural style of Venice in Italy, consisting of a colorful shopping arcade and a small boulevard. There are, on the other hand, many things to do besides shopping at The Venezia. For example, you can visit the barn with horses and sheep, go to a 3D gallery similar to Art in Paradise in Chiang Mai and Bangkok, enjoy the rides in the small amusement park, or play games in the arcade. The area also includes a small canal with classic gondolas.

Unfortunately, though, on days with few visitors, especially during the low season, some parts of the park shut down. To get the most out of a visit to The Venezia, you should go on a weekend during the high season, preferably around sunset.

Directions: The easiest way to get to The Venezia is by your own vehicle, or some kind of taxi. Alternatively, get on the red and orange local bus that runs between Hua Hin and Cha-Am. The park is about 10 kilometers north of Hua Hin on route 4.
Opening hours: Daily 10.00 – 23.30 (the opening hours vary depending on the season).
Admission fees: Combination tickets range from 50 baht to 800 baht per person depending on what you want to do in the park.

Waghor Aquarium

Just south of the provincial capital of Prachuap Khiri Khan, which is about 65 kilometers south of Hua Hin, lies Waghor Aquarium. At Waghor there are, among other things, a long underwater tunnel and several big aquariums with large panoramic windows. In addition, the visitors are treated to daily feeding shows of some of the larger sea creatures, such as the sting rays and the sharks.

The aquarium is smaller than, for example, Sea Life Bangkok Ocean World or Chiang Mai Aquarium; however, a visit to Waghor can be combined with several other fun and interesting activities, not least sightseeing. This provincial capital is often overlooked when visiting the area since Hua Hin and Cha-Am have become the big tourist magnets. Nevertheless, the fact is that Burma is only a stone's throw away, the beaches are long and child-friendly, the golf courses are cheap and excellent, and just around the corner lies a national park with cave systems and mangroves.

Directions: The easiest way to get to Waghor Aquarium is by local bus or mini bus from Hua Hin to Prachuap Khiri Khan. The ride takes approximately 90 minutes.
Opening hours: Daily 09.00 – 16.00.
Admission fees: Adults 20 baht. Children 10 baht.

Water Parks

Along the coastlines of Hua Hin and Cha-Am, there are endlessly long beaches with wonderful spots for swimming and sunbathing. Nevertheless, if you are looking for a more exiting alternative, then a visit to any of the three big water parks in the area is a must.

Black Mountain Water Park

Black Mountain Water Park consists of a large number of pools of varying sizes, as well as nine different water slides connected to a 17-meters-tall tower. The longest is a whopping 86 meters, while the shortest is wide enough to let the whole family slide down together. The pools are, in addition, as varied as the water slides. For example, there is a large pool with an intense wave machine, creating waves that are up to two meters high. Moreover, there is a water adventure land for the younger kids, a kind of bouncy castle on water for the somewhat older kids, and a spa pool for the adults, as well as a canal running through the area where you can drift along on big swim rings.

At Black Mountain Water Park, there are towels and swimming trunks for rent, and lockers to store valuables in. The restaurants in the park serve both western and Thai foods, as well as a wide range of beverages. Trained life guards are on duty throughout the day.

Directions: The easiest way to get to Black Mountain Water Park is by using the free shuttle bus, which departs from the clock tower in Hua Hin

several times a day. Black Mountain Water Park is located about 15 kilometers west of Hua Hin. Leave the city via soi 70, turn at route 3218, then turn right on route 1049, and continue for another 10 kilometers.
Opening hours: Daily 10.00 – 18.00.
Admission fees: Adults (over 140 cm) 600 baht. Children (90 cm – 139 cm) 300 baht. Free admission for children under 90 cm.

Santorini Water Fantasy

Santorini Water Fantasy is, as Vana Nava Hua Hin Water Park, a truly modern and innovative water park. The selection of water slides and pools is very varied, and among them are some of the perhaps most original in the whole of Thailand. In addition, there are plenty of shallow pools with fun activities, spouting fountains, and large playgrounds for children of all ages. The park is new and, because of that, filled with smart and state-of-the-art solutions for everything from payment systems to lockers.

There are always plenty of trained life guards on duty, making sure that parents can relax while their children are playing. As an added bonus, Santorini Water Fantasy is right next to Santorini Park.

Directions: The easiest way to get to Santorini Water Fantasy is by your own vehicle, or some kind of taxi. Alternatively, the red and orange local bus that runs between Hua Hin and Cha-Am stops right outside the entrance of Santorini Park and Santorini Water Fantasy.
Opening hours: Monday to Friday 10.00 – 19.00. Saturday and Sunday 09.00 – 19.00.
Admission fees: Adults 900 baht. Children (90 – 119 cm) 350 baht. Discounts are offered for senior citizens.

Vana Nava Hua Hin Water Park

Very close to central Hua Hin lies a more or less brand-new water park with some of the biggest slides in the whole of Asia, including a several stories high playground called The Rain Fortress. Lazy River is another favorite among the visitors – a canal with light currents that push you through small manmade caves and imageries of tropical jungles – not to mention the funnel water slides that are big enough to fit large rafts accommodating several people at a time. At Vana Nava, there is something for everyone, regardless of how brave or yellow you are.

At night-time, the place transforms into a music venue, sometimes with well-known artists. In addition, Vana Nava can also boast of having an adventure park with high climbing walls, an exciting rope course, and a modern FlowRider, similar to the one at Flow House Bangkok, generating surf waves in a sloping pool where you can use either ordinary boards or body boards. At Vana Nana, all the life guards on duty are trained and certified.

Directions: The easiest way to get to Vana Nava is by using the free shuttle bus, which departs from Hua Hin Clock Tower. Vana Nava is close to central Hua Hin, located next to soi 89.
Opening hours: Water Park daily 10.00 – 18.00. Adventure Zone daily 10.00 – 21.00.
Admission fees for the Water Park: Adults (over 122 cm) 1 000 baht. Children (91 cm – 121 cm) 600 baht. Senior citizens (over 60 years of age) 600 baht. Family package (2 adults + 2 children) 2 600 baht.
Fees for the Adventure Zone: 150 – 400 baht depending on activity.

Phuket

Phuket is the biggest island in Thailand and the landscape covering this massive area consists of steep hills and impenetrable jungles, as well as of long golden beaches and busy towns. Many of the visitors to Phuket consider the island to be a micro-cosmos of Thailand. And it does not matter what you are looking for, since you most likely will be able to find it here.

Next to Phuket lie some of the most beautiful islands in the whole of Southeast Asia. The nature of the surrounding national parks in the Andaman Sea is amazing with vibrant coral reefs, vast fish populations, thick and lush jungles, and clean and fresh waterfalls. To top it off, the colorful lime rocks shooting up from the blue sea look like something you would only be able to find on a retouched postcard.

The other side of Phuket is the buzzing night life, all the shops and the local markets, as well as the never-ending supply of bars and restaurants, along with everything else that might be associated with big city life in classic tourist spots around the world. It is easy and comfortable to spend a couple of weeks in Phuket as the locals are well-accustomed to tourists and, not least, the English language.

Animal Shows

In Phuket, as in many other tourist destinations in Thailand, there are plenty of animal shows to visit, as well as both small and big zoos. Some of these are beneath contempt, places where entertainment is everything, and the well-being of the animals nothing.

This does not mean, however, that all animal shows or zoos belong to this rather unpleasant category. At some venues, the activities geared towards the tourist market is just a means to secure funds for future rehabilitation of mishandled and abused animals. At the end of the day, it is the visitor himself of herself who must decide what to see and where to go. Nevertheless, there are several fun and exciting animal shows in Phuket and in most cases, if tickets are booked at a local travel agency, free transfer is included in the price.

In addition to the shows listed in the following sections, here are some other alternatives, if interested in animals: Phuket Monkey Show, Phuket Monkey School, Phuket Crocodile Show, Phuket Snake Farm, Phuket Cobra Show, and Phuket Zoo. However, as mentioned above, some of these might not be on par with western standards.

Elephant Trekking

The coastline of Phuket consists of kilometer after kilometer of powder-like beaches suitable for both adults and children; however, a bit further inland you will find a kind of nature that is just as wild as the jungle mountains of northern Thailand, which has led many local travel agencies to start arranging elephant treks.

All sorts of different kinds of trips and treks are offered, often in combination with other fun and exciting activities, such as swimming in waterfalls, snorkeling, picnics, or perhaps white water rafting. Keep in mind, though, that considering the large number of offered treks on the market, you should shop around a bit before deciding what to do, and how much to pay.

Directions: Most local travel agencies can arrange elephant treks with free transfer to and from the guests' hotels included in the price.
Opening hours: From morning to night all year round.
Fees: The cost of a trek usually starts at around 800 baht.

Fishing

Phuket is an island, thereby offering great opportunities for both fishing and boating. If you decide to go on a boat trip to fish, bear in mind that this can only be done comfortably during the high season between November and May, since it is too dangerous to head out during the yearly monsoons. In addition, most boat trips can be combined with swimming and snorkeling at any of the small islands in the marine national parks of greater Phuket. A multitude of local travel agencies arrange deep sea fishing along with other fun and exciting activities.

If you, on the other hand, opt to do some freshwater fishing, then you can fish all year round. In Phuket, there are quite a few artificial lakes to choose between, but one of the best, and perhaps biggest, is AC's Phuket Fishing Park. At AC's, both professionals and absolute beginners are welcome, since the lake has been divided into various sections with different species of fish, where the biggest can weigh up to 100 kilograms.

Directions: The easiest way to get to AC's Fishing Park in Sawai Lake is by your own vehicle, or some kind of taxi. The park is located in the north of Phuket. If travelling from Phuket town, take route 402, Thepkrasattri Road, to soi 30.
Opening hours: Tuesday to Sunday 07.30 – 17.00 (the opening hours will vary depending on the season).
Fees: The cost starts at around 800 baht per person, and rise according to the size of the fish you plan to catch.

Horse Riding

To ride in Thailand, whether it is on a jungle trek or along the beaches at sunset, is something everyone in the family will be able to thoroughly enjoy together. In Phuket, there are a number of small stables located in the vicinity of most beaches. One of the biggest and best run, though, is Phuket International Horse Club.

Phuket International Horse Club

Phuket International Horse Club offers horseback riding on the beach for both absolute beginners and professionals. They have a wide range of horses and ponies in order to suit all kinds of riders.

The horse club is open all day long; however, the most popular trips are in the morning at sunrise, and in the evening at sunset. You also have the option of exploring nearby Layan National Park on horseback. In addition to excursions, trips, and sunset rides, Phuket International Horse Club offers riding lessons for riders at all levels. Most of the rides take place on or around Laguna Beach.

Directions: The easiest way to get to Laguna Beach in the northwest of Phuket is by your own vehicle, or some kind of taxi. It is also possible to arrange trips with free transfer through local travel agencies.
Opening hours: Daily 08.00 – 18.30.
Fees: Horse rides start at around 1 000 baht per hour and person.

Island Hopping

In Phuket, there is a multitude of exciting and fun trips for anyone in the family who is interested in diving, surfing, or snorkeling. Whether you are staying in Phuket Town or at any of the beaches, for example, Patong, Kata or Laguna, you can book anything from full diving certificate courses to sunbathing trips to Phang Nga Bay.

Kayaking is another very popular way of exploring the surrounding marine parks and islands. And there are many islands to explore. Just to name a few: Similan Island, Coral Island, Racha Island, Coconut Island, Koh Yao Nai, Koh Lone, Koh Sirey, Koh Khai Nok, and the backpacker favorite Koh Phi Phi. In addition, you will find one of the biggest islands in Thailand just south of Phuket, namely Koh Lanta, which is like a smaller and much quieter version of Phuket. Just remember that island hoping is not a very good idea during the monsoon season.

Kids Club Phuket / Kee Resort and Spa

Sometimes it can be nice to avoid the heat and the salty sea for a while, and this is easily done in the new mall of Kee Plaza. Here there is something for everyone, especially for parents who want to indulge in a bit of luxury and some alone time.

At Kee Plaza, they have a big Kids Club, where the children can play and be entertained while mum and dad go to the spa, or stroll around the luxurious shopping complex. There is another Kids Club located on the Promenade at Patong, not far from Kee Resort. However, the Promenade recently underwent renovations, so it might be a good idea to check the Facebook page of the company first to see if they have reopened yet.

Directions: The easiest way to get to both Kee Plaza and the Promenade is on foot, since both locations are within walking distance of Patong Beach.
Opening hours: Daily 10.00 – 21.00.
Admission fees: The fee starts at around 100 – 200 baht per hour and child.

Mini-Golf in Phuket

In Phuket, there are several fun and exciting options if you feel like taking your family for a game of mini-golf.

Mini-Golf at Dino Park

Mini Golf at Dino Park is an 18-hole course that is so much more than just a game of golf – it is an entire experience! The area has been constructed in the form of a theme park with dinosaurs that both move and make sounds.

Moreover, there is a twelve-meter-high waterfall along the course, as well as a small volcano that erupts every thirty minutes. The ambience is enhanced by smoke machines and sound and light effects. This means that a visit to Dino Park is, by far, most entertaining after sun set. To make the most of it you could always have dinner at the restaurant in the park, where everything, including the outfits of the staff, follows the dinosaur theme.

Directions: The easiest way to get to Mini-Golf at Dino Park is by your own vehicle, or some kind of taxi. Mini-Golf at Dino Park is located on Beach Road between Kata Beach and Karon Beach.
Opening hours: Daily 10.00 – 23.00.
Fees: Adults (over 12 years old) 240 baht per person. Children (4 – 11 years old) 180 baht per person.

Football Crazy Golf

A fun alternative to an ordinary round of mini-golf is Football Crazy Golf. Just as with a normal golf course, there are 18 holes to complete, however, with the big difference that you are using footballs instead of golf balls. And you have to, as their slogan says, *"bend it like Beckham"*, to get the ball in the hole.

The golf course is ideally located for a combination of activities, as you can find places like Tiger Kingdom and Patong Go-Cart Speedway nearby.

Directions: The easiest way to get to Football Crazy Golf is by your own vehicle, or some kind of taxi. The course is situated along route 4029, Vichitsongkram Road, which starts at Patong Beach.
Opening hours: Daily 09.00 – 19.00.
Fees: Adults 700 baht. Children 400 baht.

Phuket Adventure Mini-Golf

Phuket Adventure Mini-Golf is first and foremost a combination of a mini-golf course and a putting course, suitable for both adults and children. The holes and lawns are well-kept and of a very high standard. In addition, the landscaped area is very beautiful and the restaurant excellent, with both western and Thai dishes on the menu.

The golf course is located right next to the beach, which means that you can combine a trip to Phuket Adventure Mini-Golf with swimming and sunbathing.

Directions: The easiest way to get to Phuket Adventure Mini-Golf is by your own vehicle, or some kind of taxi. The golf course is right next to Bangtao Beach at Bangtao Beach Road soi 2.
Opening hours: Daily 11.00 – 23.00.
Fees: Adults play all day for 700 baht (one drink included). Children play all day for 500 baht (one drink included).

Museums in Phuket

At times, one can get too much of beach life, swimming, trekking through jungles, and other kinds of outdoor activities. If so, there are three museums to visit in Phuket, more or less free of charge.

Thalang National Museum

At Thalang National Museum, you can take part of the history of Phuket and the local communities along the coastline of the Andaman Sea. All the various and differing ethnic groups that have occupied the area are described along with their culture, customs, and traditions. The museum also contains much information about Phuket of today.

Directions: The easiest way to get to Thalang National Museum is by your own vehicle, or some kind of taxi. Drive north from Phuket Town on route 402, turn right on route 4027, and then make another right towards the Heroines' Monument on Pa Khlok Road.
Opening hours: Daily 09.00 – 16.00.
Admission fees: No admission fees.

Phuket Mining Museum in Kathu

Phuket used to be the center of Thailand's mining industry and tin production, and the hard labor was usually carried out by Chinese immigrants.

At Phuket Mining Museum, they have recreated the past through a series of impressive displays, ranging from miniature figures situated in realistic landscapes to life size dolls placed in genuine job stations.

Directions: The easiest way to get to Phuket Mining Museum is by your own vehicle, or some kind of taxi. The museum is located along route 3030, about three kilometers south of the British International School.
Opening hours: Monday to Saturday 08.00 – 16.00.
Admission fees: There is a very small entrance fee.

Phuket Seashell Museum

At Phuket Seashell Museum, you will find some of the most sought-after and valuable seashells in the world. Moreover, there are pearl exhibitions boasting, among other things, the world's biggest pearl, fossils from various geological time periods, and enormous seashells weighing up to 140 kilograms.

As an added bonus, the souvenir shop is unusually intriguing.

Directions: The easiest way to get to Phuket Seashell Museum is by your own vehicle, or some kind of taxi. The museum is located in the south of Phuket, along route 4024, almost all the way down to Rawai Beach.
Opening hours: Daily 08.00 – 18.00.
Admission fees: There is a very small entrance fee.

Paramotor Flying Phuket

One of the most exciting things to do when on a holiday in Thailand is paramotor flying. A paramotor is a small airplane with three wheels, a rotor blade at the back, as well as a kind of parachute attached to the top. The plane takes off by the aid of the propeller, and then gently sails through the air at the chosen altitude. Paramotor Flying is considered to be one of the safest ways of flying, since you are flying at a low speed, and not too high up in the air. The company's slogan, *"Flying Low and Slow"*, sums up the experience nicely.

Only qualified staff work at Paramotor Flying Phuket, certified by both European and American organizations. The actual flying is carried out with two people sitting in the aircraft, the paying customer and the flight instructor, who is maneuvering the plane. No prior experience is needed, and there is no age limit. The activity is open to everyone who is not scared of heights.

Directions: The easiest way to get to Phuket Airpark is by your own vehicle, or some kind of taxi. The office, Sky Club Asia, is located about 20 kilometers north of Phuket Town. Follow route 402 to route 4027, and then continue for another couple of kilometers. Flights, however, are usually booked over the Internet or via local travel agencies.
Opening hours: Daily from early morning to late night.

Fees: A standard trip with an accompanying instructor starts at 4 600 baht per person.

Patong Go-Kart Speed Way

At Patong Go-Kart Speedway, there are vehicles for everybody in the family. The ones with the smallest engines have a top speed of 40 km/h, while the fastest ones can reach a top speed of a whopping 110 km/h. There are also go-karts with passenger seats, so that the youngest members of the family can go for a ride with their parents.

The track is 750 meters long and in the middle of it lies a restaurant, allowing you to follow the action while having a bite to eat. Furthermore, the management has also constructed a 600-meter-long off-road track for Beach Buggies, where you force your way through and over all sorts of natural obstacles. No prior experience is needed, however, there might be an age restriction. As an added bonus, competitions are regularly arranged at Patong Go-Kart Speedway, who anyone can participate in.

Directions: The easiest way to get to Patong Go-Kart Speedway is by your own vehicle, or some kind of taxi. The tracks are located along route 4029, Vichitsongkram Road, which begins at Patong Beach.
Opening hours: Daily 10.00 – 19.00.
Fees: The cost starts at around 800 baht per person for 15 – 30 minutes.

Phuket Aquarium

Recently, Phuket Aquarium underwent major renovations, turning it into something much more than just an aquarium. Now they can boast a wide range of activities and displays, not least an underwater glass tunnel where you can observe all sorts of sea creatures, including huge stingrays and sharks.

In addition, Phuket Aquarium cooperates with Phuket Marine Biological Center (PMBC), and after a visit to the actual aquarium, you can continue to the area of PMBC. Along the pathway from Phuket Aquarium, you will come across several large pools where PMBC breeds endangered fish and giant sea turtles, which later will be released into the sea.

Close by is the research ship of PMBC, and visitors have the opportunity to climb on board and learn more about how to catch, raise, breed, and release endangered sea creatures. A trip to Phuket Aquarium and PMBC is the perfect excursion on a rainy day.

Directions: The easiest way to get to Phuket Aquarium is by your own vehicle, or some kind of taxi. The aquarium is located south of Phuket Town, at the end of Cape Panwa, along route 4129.
Opening hours: Daily 08.30 – 16.30.
Admission fees: Adults 180 baht. Children 100 baht.

Phuket Bird Park

At Phuket Bird Park, you will find birds of various shapes, colors, and sizes from several continents. The area is big and spacious, offering great opportunities for taking pictures of yourself with the birds. Visitors to Phuket Bird Park are also allowed to feed the birds, which is a highly anticipated event by the birds. Many of the smaller ones literally cover peoples' arms and shoulders in a bid to get hold of some seeds.

One of the main attractions of the park are the daily shows, where different species of birds perform all kinds of complicated tricks and stunts.

Directions: The easiest way to get to Phuket Bird Park is by your own vehicle, or some kind of taxi. The park is located between Kata/Karon Beach and Phuket Town, along road 4021, Chai Fah Tawan Tok Road.
Opening hours: Daily 09.00 – 17.00. Shows are put on three times a day.
Admission fees: 500 baht for adults. 300 baht for children under the age of 12.

Asia Revealed Publishing Company

Phuket FantaSea

Close to Kamala Beach lies Phuket FantaSea, which is marketed as the ultimate culture theme park in true Las Vegas style. The main attraction at this spectacular park in central Kamala is an enormous stage with elephants, acrobats, and several hundred artists putting on a show about the history of Thailand with a truly sparkling and dazzling touch.

The show starts late in the evening. However, before getting seated, there is plenty of time to enjoy a first-class dinner buffet in one of the biggest restaurants in the world. At Phuket FantaSea, you will also find an amusement park called The Similian Entertainment Center. Moreover, there are plenty of good shopping venues at the Carnival Village Shopping Street, as well as a so-called Theater Safari with impressive sound, light, and screen effects. Phuket FantaSea puts on one of the biggest, grandest, and most extravagant shows in the world, and it is well-recommended after a long day at the beach.

Directions: The easiest way to get to Phuket FantaSea is by the shuttle bus service of the park, which costs 300 baht per person. The venue is within walking distance for guests living close to Kamala Beach.
Opening hours: Friday to Wednesday 17.30 – 23.30.
Admission fees for the show: Adults and children 1 800 baht per person.
Admission fees for the show with dinner buffet: Adults 2 200 baht. Children (ages 4 – 12) 2 000 baht.

Phuket Trickeye Museum

Phuket Trickeye Museum is a gallery with interactive 3D paintings; however, not in the form of holograms, but in the guise of actual paintings. What it is about is creating the illusion of the beholder stepping into the artwork. The paintings are huge, sometimes covering entire walls, and offer amazing photo opportunities where oneself becomes part of the motif.

Next to most of the paintings, there are instructions on how you should position yourself to best create the impression of being an integral part of the composition. The optical illusions are stunning and the whole family will be fascinated by the end result when captured by your own camera.

As with the other 3D galleries mentioned in this book, which are more or less identical in concept, a visit to Phuket Trickeye Museum is easily combined with other fun activities due to its central location.

Directions: The easiest way to get to Phuket Trickeye Museum is on foot, or by some kind of taxi. The 3D gallery is located at the corner of Montri and Phang Nga Road in Phuket Town.
Opening hours: Daily 10.00 – 19.00.
Admission fees: Adults 450 baht. Children (under 130 cm) 270 baht.

Shopping Malls

In Phuket, there are several modern shopping malls where you can find everything from cheap Thai products to some of the most exclusive brand names available. However, there are only two shopping malls that also cater to the interests of children and teenagers.

Jungceylon Shopping Mall

Jungceylon Shopping Mall is the newest, biggest and by far the most fashionable shopping mall in the whole of southern Thailand, lavished with daily light, sound, and water shows. At Jungceylon, you can easily spend the whole day and, not least, the whole night, since there is a multitude of bars, restaurants, nightclubs, and concert venues scattered all over the place.

Furthermore, at Jungceylon you will also find state-of-the-art bowling alleys and cinemas, including a 4D cinema, gaming arcades, fish spas, massage parlors, and so much more. For the younger children, there are the playlands of Molly Fantasy and Kidzoona, where the kids can play for hours while being supervised by trained staff. Molly Fantasy and Kidzoona can also be found in Bangkok, where the biggest branch is located in the shopping mall Gateway Ekkamai.

Directions: The easiest way to get to Jungceylon Shopping Mall is on foot as it is located in central Patong.
Opening hours: Daily 10.00 – 23.00.
Admission fees: There is no admission fee for Jungceylon Shopping Mall. However, Molly Fantasy and Kidzoona cost, and the price starts at around 100 – 200 baht per child.

Central Festival Phuket

The shopping mall Central Festival Phuket is somewhat older than Jungceylon, although still modern enough with excellent shopping venues and many bowling alleys, cinemas, gaming arcades, restaurants, cafés, and ice-cream parlors.

On one of the four floors, they have created a vast space called Eduplanet at Central Festival. At Eduplanet, there is much to do and to explore, especially for children who are creative and enjoy music and various forms of arts and crafts. Two of the best places to visit at Eduplanet is Hands on Art Studio, and Lekanoi Craftz – perfect options for parents who would like to go shopping on their own, or perhaps enjoy a massage in peace and quiet.

Directions: The easiest way to get to Central Festival Phuket is by your own vehicle, or some kind of taxi. The shopping mall is located west of Phuket Town, at the intersection of route 4020 and route 402.
Opening hours: Daily 10.30 – 22.00.
Admission fees: There is no admission fee for the shopping mall. All the activities at Eduplanet will, on the other hand, cost.

Siam Niramit Show

One of the biggest shows in the world is Siam Niramit, which can be found in both Bangkok and Phuket. Over one hundred actors, changing costumes up to five hundred times, take part in the show. The show itself is about Thailand and comes in three acts. In act one, the audience is informed about the four geographical areas that Thailand has been divided into and how they have evolved during the last 700 years. In act two, Thai belief systems, myths, and folklores are enacted. In act three, all the different customs and festivals which make up the core of what one might call *"Thainess"* is brought to life on stage. However, this is not your normal theater production, but rather a grand spectacle with impressive special effects and extravagant props.

A couple of hours before the start of every show, the audience is invited to try out, and take part in, various local customs, such as playing classical instruments, make batik, and bake delicacies.

Directions: The easiest way to get to Siam Niramit is by using the free shuttle bus service of the company. The theater is located approximately 8 kilometers north of Phuket Town, between route 402 and route 3001.
Opening hours: The show starts daily at 20.00 and lasts for about 80 minutes. Additional activities start at 17.30.
Admission fees for the show: 1 500 – 2 000 baht depending on seating arrangements.
Admission fees for the show with dinner: 1 720 – 2 350 baht depending on seating arrangements.

Splash Jungle Water Park

The biggest water park in southern Thailand is Splash Jungle Water Park. The park covers a vast area and consists of a total of twelve water slides, some of which are really steep, fast and, not least, original. In addition, there are several small and big pools to swim and play around in, including a large wave pool.

As in many other water parks around Thailand, at Splash Jungle Water park you will find a so-called Lazy River, with a length of 400 meters, where you can drift along on giant swim rings. For the younger children, there are playgrounds with slides, water cannons, fountains, and all sorts of other fun things. As an added bonus, the beach is just a stone's throw away, making it possible to switch from pool water to sea water whenever you feel like it.

Directions: The easiest way to get to Splash Jungle Water Park is by using the free shuttle bus service of the park. Splash Jungle Water Park is located north of the airport, next to Centara Grand West Sand Resort at Mai Khao Beach.
Opening hours: Daily 10.00 – 18.00.
Admission fees: 1 295 baht for adults and 650 baht for children between ages 5 and 12. Free admission for children under the age of 5.

Surf House Phuket

Right next to Kata Beach lies Surf House Phuket, where you can surf every day without having to worry about the weather. The FlowRider at Surf House Phuket is the biggest and newest in the whole of southern Thailand, which means that the level of difficulty can be adjusted to suit both beginners and advanced surfers (the minimum recommended age, though, is 6 years old).

It is possible to switch the surfboard to a bodyboard, which tends to be the most popular choice among young surfers. Since Surf House Phuket is located by the beach, you can swim and sunbathe as much as you want before or after surfing. Besides providing a state-of-the-art FlowRider, the management at Surf House Phuket has also done their best to create a genuine Californian atmosphere, topped off by their all-American menu.

Directions: The easiest way to get to Surf House Phuket is by your own vehicle, on foot, or some kind of taxi. Surf House Phuket is located at the southern end of Kata Beach.
Opening hours: Daily from early morning to late night.
Fees: Surfing starts at around 800 baht per hour (discounts are available).

Tiger Kingdom Phuket

Tiger Kingdom in Phuket is a branch of Tiger Kingdom in the province of Ubon Rachathani in the northeast of the country, where it is known as Ubon Zoo. At Tiger Kingdom Phuket, a large number of tigers have been born and bred on the premises. Each tiger has been reared by a personal trainer, which raises certain moral issues since that prevents the tigers from ever being released into the wild at an adult age. The tigers at Tiger Kingdom have been domesticated to such a high degree that it is possible for visitors to enter their compounds to touch and take photos.

The area is big and as a guest you only book the pens and tigers that you wish to visit, usually for ten minutes at a time. Although calm and docile, the larger tigers can be truly intimidating, while the tiger cubs are just as playful as ordinary cats. The trainers are always present, which is comforting since there are no fences separating the visitors from the tigers once you have entered their pens.

At the present, following requirements are in effect:

1. To *meet the big tigers, the visitor must be at least 18 years old and 160 centimeters tall*
2. To *meet the middle-sized tigers, the visitor must be at least 15 years old and 160 centimeters tall*
3. To *meet the small tigers, the visitor must be at least 140 centimeters tall*
4. To *meet the white tigers, the visitor must be at least 150 centimeters tall*
5. *There are no requirements for meeting the tiger cubs*

Directions: The easiest way to get to Tiger Kingdom Phuket is by your own vehicle, or some kind of taxi. The park is located along route 4029, Vichitsongkram Road, which begins at Patong Beach.
Opening hours: Daily 09.00 – 18.00.
Admission fees: The fee is based on the number of tigers you want to visit, as well as on the size of them. A visit will probably cost 500 – 1 000 baht per person. Discounts are available.

Upside-Down House: Baan Teelanka

In Phuket town, there is a highly unusual attraction, namely a completely upside-down house which, in addition, comes with a complex garden labyrinth to explore, as well as two "Escape the Room" adventures.

And yes, Baan Teelanka is exactly what the label says it is: a house that has been built with the roof resting on the ground, and the floor reaching for the sky. A host of weird and wonderful photo opportunities are offered. And once done strolling around the Upside-Down House, there is still plenty of time to try out the other activities.

Directions: The easiest way to get to the Upside-Down House Baan Teelanka is by your own vehicle, or some kind of taxi. Baan Teelanka is located a couple of kilometers north of Phuket Town on route 402, between Siam Niramit and Premium Outlet.
Opening hours: Daily 10.00 – 18.00.
Admission fees for the Upside-Down House: Adults 290 baht. Children 170 baht.
Admission fees for the Garden Labyrinth: Adults 150 baht. Children 100 baht.

Wakeboarding

If you like water skiing, then wakeboarding might be something for you, and since you do not follow a boat out at sea, but instead hook yourself up to a cable system at a lake, this is an activity that can be enjoyed all year round. Although no prior experience is needed it might, however, be a bit too physically demanding for the youngest members of the family.

Phuket Wake Park

Phuket Wake Park is of a very high standard and markets itself as the best wakeboard park in Asia. Its 700-meter-long cable system allows rider to reach really high speeds; however, the courses have been built to suit professionals looking for a real challenge as well as absolute beginners.

In the Park, there is a large restaurant and a swimming pool, where you can relax and go for a swim both before and after wakeboarding. The park also comes with its own bungalow hotel.

Directions: The easiest way to get to Phuket Wake Park is by your own vehicle, or some kind of taxi. The park is located at the end of Soi Namtok Kathu, which is reached by route 4029, Vichitsongkram Road.
Opening hours: Daily 07.30 – 22.00.
Fees: The price starts at 300 baht per person for beginners and children. For adults with previous experience, the price starts at 650 baht.

Anthem Wake Park

The wakeboard park of Anthem is considered to be unique since the cable system moves in a clockwise direction, and also because it is situated at a completely natural lake. The freshwater does not contain any chemicals at all, and is continually replenished by the water running off the surrounding jungle hills.

There are two systems available at the present, one for beginners and another one for professionals. The beginner's course is somewhat shorter, while the course for advanced wakeboarders is about 650 meters long, with numerous jumps. The ambition at Anthem Wake Park is to attract the elite in the sport.

Directions: The easiest way to get to Anthem Wake Park is by your own vehicle, or some kind of taxi. The park is located between the airport and Phuket Town. Take route 402 to route 4025, Si Sunthon Road, turn west on route 4025, and then head south at The Manic Temple Gate.
Opening hours: Daily 09.00 – 18.30.
Fees: The cost starts at 400 baht per child, and at 800 baht per adult.

White Water Rafting

White water rafting might not be for everyone in the family; however, if brave enough, you will experience a true adventure. Moreover, the options available in Phuket are really varied, both when it comes to the level of difficulty and the kind of nature you wish to explore. Excursions to the mountainous hills of Phuket, or into its dense jungles, can often be combined with other activities, for example, nice picnics, swimming in waterfalls, elephant trekking, or jungle trekking on ATVs.

A much-appreciated alternative is white water rafting in the nearby national park of Phang Nga, which is only accessible by boat. There are many tour companies operating in the market, meaning that you should shop around a bit before putting together a trip.

Directions: Most local travel agencies and hotels will offer white water rafting with free transfer to and from any hotel in Phuket.
Opening hours: From morning to night all year round, although depending on the weather.
Fees: White water rafting usually starts at around 800 – 1 000 baht per person. Discounts are available when combining activities.

Ziplining: Flying Hanuman & Jungle Xtrem Adventure Park

Ziplining is an activity that has grown steadily in Thailand during the last couple of years, which might not be so surprising since the jungle canopies are well-suited for elevated courses. In Phuket there are large areas of more or less untouched wilderness, making it ideal for ziplining among the treetops, from platform to platform, in combination with short walks over suspension bridges made out of wood. It might seem scary, but the zipline courses in Phuket are of a high international standard with certified safety equipment.

In Phuket, there are two big and long courses to choose between, the Flying Hanuman, and Jungle Xtrem Adventure Park. Both parks suit participants of all ages. However, Jungle Xtrem Adventure Park has put a bit more effort into creating courses for children.

Directions to the Flying Hanuman: The easiest way to get to the Flying Hanuman is by your own vehicle, or some kind of taxi. The course is located along the road to Kathu Waterfalls at Soi Namtok Kathu, which is reached via route 4029, Vichitsongkram Road.
Opening hours: Daily 08.00 – 18.00.
Fees: The price starts at around 2 000 baht per person.
Directions to Jungle Xtrem Adventure Park: The easiest way to get to Jungle Xtrem Adventure Park is by using the free shuttle bus service of the company. The park is located between Karon Beach and Phuket Town along Jaofa Road, which it reached by route 4021.
Opening hours: Daily 09.00 – 18.00.
Fees: The cost starts at around 900 baht per child, and at around 1 900 baht per adult.

Zorbing at Rollerball

A so-called Zorb, or rollerball, is a gigantic inflatable ball with enough space in the middle of it to carry up to two persons, and in which you can roll over both land and water. This activity can be enjoyed all over Thailand at most tourist destinations; however, at Zorbing at Rollerball you will find one of the absolutely longest roller ball hills in the entire world.

The Zorbs used are not ordinary either, but come in many different styles and sizes. For example, there are tandem balls, in case you do not want to roll by yourself, and Zorb balls filled with water in which you can splash around while darting down the long course.

Directions: The easiest way to get to Zorbing at Rollerball, located at soi 7 near Kalim Beach, is by your own vehicle, or some kind of taxi. However, if you are staying in or around Patong and Kalim beach, the staff can pick you up at your hotel.

Opening hours: Daily from 10.00 to late.

Fees: The cost starts at around 950 baht per person. Big discounts are offered for multiple runs.

www.ingramcontent.com/pod-product-compliance
Lightning Source LLC
Chambersburg PA
CBHW071009080526
44587CB00015B/2399